Kinga Szabó-Tóth

Social Innovation and Higher Education
From Theory to Practice

Kinga Szabó-Tóth

SOCIAL INNOVATION AND HIGHER EDUCATION

From Theory to Practice

Bibliografische Information der Deutschen Nationalbibliothek
Die Deutsche Nationalbibliothek verzeichnet diese Publikation in der Deutschen Nationalbibliografie; detaillierte bibliografische Daten sind im Internet über http://dnb.d-nb.de abrufbar.

Bibliographic information published by the Deutsche Nationalbibliothek
The Deutsche Nationalbibliothek lists this publication in the Deutsche Nationalbibliografie; detailed bibliographic data are available on the Internet at http://dnb.d-nb.de.

Lector: György Csepeli

ISBN (Print): 978-3-8382-1684-3
ISBN (E-Book [PDF]): 978-3-8382-7684-7
© *ibidem*-Verlag, Hannover • Stuttgart 2025

Alle Rechte vorbehalten

Leuschnerstraße 40
30457 Hannover
info@ibidem.eu

Das Werk einschließlich aller seiner Teile ist urheberrechtlich geschützt. Jede Verwertung außerhalb der engen Grenzen des Urheberrechtsgesetzes ist ohne Zustimmung des Verlages unzulässig und strafbar. Dies gilt insbesondere für Vervielfältigungen, Übersetzungen, Mikroverfilmungen und elektronische Speicherformen sowie die Einspeicherung und Verarbeitung in elektronischen Systemen.

All rights reserved. No part of this publication may be reproduced, stored in or introduced into a retrieval system, or transmitted, in any form, or by any means (electronic, mechanical, photocopying, recording or otherwise) without the prior written permission of the publisher. Any person who commits any unauthorized act in relation to this publication may be liable to criminal prosecution and civil claims for damages.

Printed in the EU

Content

Foreword 7

Chapter 1 The Concept, Models and Measurement of Social Innovation 11

Chapter 2 Applied Social Science Research and Social Innovation 25

Chapter 3 Design Thinking, "Wicked" Problems and Social Innovation: From Theory to Practice 41

Chapter 4 Higher Education and Social Responsibility 59

Chapter 5 The Role of Community Coaching in Social Innovation Projects 73

Chapter 6 Case Studies 85

   6.1. Predicting and Managing Local Conflicts in the Framework of a Social Innovation Project 85

   6.2. "Creative Region" – Using Innovation to Reduce Regional Disadvantages 98

   6.3. Local Innovation Potential – The Basic Model and Its Testing 108

   6.4. Social Innovation for Active Ageing 125

   6.5. Promoting the Integration of People in Deprived Districts Through a Social Innovation Pilot Project 140

Foreword

Since the end of the 20th century, we have been increasingly confronted — both as researchers and as individuals — with a great number of impacts that are not local but global, worldwide. And we cannot possibly hide away from them. With a slight exaggeration, we may say that there is no shelter from them in any corner of the world (let us think of COVID-19, the world accelerating, the challenges of ageing societies and generational differences, and the fact that the world is becoming highly polarised, with the social, economic and territorial inequalities posing a major challenge for regions, countries, decision-makers — not least those who suffer the most). Modernity entails global risks that can significantly undermine our need for security. These risks or challenges are extended both spatially and temporally and are difficult to decipher. They increasingly take the form of so-called "wild problems," which we have no mysterious formula or perfect recipe for and, quite likely, no single optimal solution to.

Accordingly, in the 21st century, social sciences, and sociology in particular, faced the challenge of having to reassess their role, that is, finding their place among these phenomena, which are often unpredictable and unforeseeable, which means taking on the task of describing, explaining, predicting or even intervening in them.

Increasing territorial and social disadvantages, lagging regions and municipalities, the drastic deterioration of the quality of life of the people living there, economic processes and sustainability issues (including environmental sustainability) are matters that frequently generate wide public debates in society and, concurrently, necessitate social collaboration. In addition, relevant research makes it increasingly clear that reducing disadvantages and overcoming deficits requires a wealth of creativity, problem-solving, design thinking and innovation.

Therefore, recent years have seen a growing focus on social innovations that can respond to these challenges in a complex way. The introduction, maintenance and management of social innovations and the processes of renewal in social sciences can converge in the notion that the elaboration and management of innovations presuppose a certain applied social science mindset.

The above phenomena greatly impact various segments or subsystems of society. These impacts are experienced at the level of higher education institutions as well, prompting their social responsibility and building on their role as catalysts. Thus, according to some theories, the ideal university of the late 20th and early 21st century is the so-called "third generation university," which realises a synergy of education, research and social responsibility (or third mission, as it is usually referred to).

I have been working as a researcher, sociologist, social worker, community developer and coach for years (decades), in addition to being the head of and teaching at the Institute of Applied Social Sciences at the Faculty of Humanities and Social Sciences, University of Miskolc (Hungary). In the past 10 years, I have been increasingly working on social innovations, in interdisciplinary and international research environments, and applying the approaches, paradigms and methods of sociology in so-called applied sociological research. In addition, and parallel to these, since I have been working in higher education for 25 years, I have also become interested in the social responsibility of higher education institutions, their so-called "third mission."

On that account, as I am involved predominantly in social innovation projects, I participate in research on social innovation and do so in a higher education context—it is these two areas that shall be linked in this book.

The aim of the present volume is thus to fill a gap by linking the fields of social innovation and higher education, and thereby facilitate reflection for stakeholders of higher education, innovation practitioners, policymakers and the general public interested in this subject matter.

The book consists of two main parts. The five chapters of the first major unit intend to shed light on the link between social innovation and higher education. Chapter 1 provides an overview of the conceptual framework and methodology of social innovation, followed by a chapter discussing and analysing the role of applied social science in generating and managing innovation. The third chapter focuses on possible solutions to a new type of challenge, "wild problems," through the presentation of innovative methods. Chapter 4 examines the primary issue of the book: social innovations and the third mission role and activity of higher education institutions. The final chapter in this part explores another novel issue: the potential of community coaching for, as well as its methods and applications in innovative projects.

The second part introduces the reader to the practice of social innovation through five case studies, all of which present projects that built heavily on the social responsibility of higher education institutions, that is, all of them were implemented in a higher education setting. Thus, these case studies describe the implementation of projects that may be models for linking the two areas. Each of the five case studies offers an insight into a different field. The first presents a project that proposes an innovative solution for identifying and then transforming social conflicts in a forward-looking way. The second describes a multi-year research and innovation project in which an interdisciplinary team developed and implemented a social innovation model in a disadvantaged region to increase its visibility, reduce its disadvantages and improve the quality of life of its inhabitants.

The third case study presents a method developed and tested in practice to measure local innovation potential. The fourth one discusses an innovative community development project for active ageing, which responds to the challenges of an ageing society, as mentioned above. Finally, the last chapter introduces an innovative international project using the methods of community coaching to develop and implement an expandable model of integrated service provision in deprived neighbourhoods, providing targeted coordination of social and employment services for disadvantaged residents.

I wish you fruitful collective thinking!

Miskolc, November, 2024
Kinga Szabó-Tóth

Chapter 1
The Concept, Models and Measurement of Social Innovation

Results of scientific research into territorial and social processes have demonstrated that disadvantages may only be reduced through the development and dissemination of innovations, particularly social ones. Unlike technical and technological innovations, social innovations characteristically focus on renewing human potential, are not created in specific research laboratories but in everyday workshops, their theory is formulated based on practical experience and they require large-scale social cooperation. In the 21st century, social sciences, and sociology in particular — both in constant need of renewal — face the challenge of their necessary involvement in developing social innovations.

But what is social innovation? Schumpeter's classic theory (1934) links innovation to economic development and the preservation of economic competitiveness. The theory deals with various forms of innovation, such as introducing a new product or a new quality of a product, using a new production technology and opening up a new market, as well as the emergence of new sources of supply, and the introduction of a new organisational form in an industry. These are all designed to describe economic innovations but are mostly applicable to social innovations as well.

The issue of social innovation has been a central theme for social researchers since the early 2000s. This is largely due to the emergence of new social and economic challenges, such as ageing societies, the digital divide, regional disparities, the deteriorating quality of life, climate change, environmental issues and inadequate responses to the needs of socially vulnerable populations, which cannot be overcome by traditional thinking and solutions (ECDG, 2006). The issue of reducing regional disparities and facilitating the catching-up process of so-called convergence regions was a critical issue during the enlargement of the EU. It also became increasingly clear that, in addition to state and local government intervention, supporting and encouraging grassroots initiatives are vital elements of the catching-up process and improving the quality of life of the inhabitants of disadvantaged areas.

Returning to the question posed above, broadly speaking social innovation can be linked to efforts to improve a community's well-being and quality of life. Other important elements of the definition include emphasis on community solutions and participation, and the novelty of the innovation itself, based on the interconnection and interaction of different sectors (public, non-profit, church).

Social innovation is often aimed at changing the status quo, which requires an innovative and problem-solving mindset. An innovative initiative or product may come in various ways and forms. Yet, identifying the problem and its causes, then critiquing existing solutions and ways of thinking, finding areas where intervention is needed, then taking action and finally evaluating are always integral parts of the process. Social innovation can take many forms: it can be a strategy, a concept, an idea or some kind of know-how, an organisational structure, a form of collaboration or a project-based initiative.

The present chapter outlines the concepts and models developed for social innovation and the methods for assessing the innovation potential of a territorial unit (region, country, municipality or part of a municipality).

Concepts and models

Although, as mentioned in the introduction, social innovation has been a very popular research topic in the past 20 years, there is still no single definition to rely on. The term was first used by two social scientists at the turn of the 19th and 20th centuries, Emile Durkheim and Max Weber, who believed that social innovations played a major role in bringing about social and technological change (Baturina–Bezovan, 2015).

Following Schumpeter's theory discussed above, the issue of social innovation was relegated to the background until the late 1990s. In fact, it is from this point on that this issue becomes highly important, as signalled by the emergence of the idea that technological and social innovation cannot be separated, as the former requires the latter to be created.

The first decade of the 2000s saw the emergence of various theories and questions, such as the relationship between design thinking (discussed in more detail in this book) and social innovation and the difference between technical, technological, economic and social innovation (Bogdány et al, 2023).

According to the OECD, social innovation does not aim to create new forms of production or to open up new markets but to provide new opportunities for meeting social needs and integrating the population into production (OECD, 2016). Social innovation brings a new practice or approach to explaining social processes and contributes to solving societal challenges.

Research on social enterprises started in 2008, due to an increasing emphasis on creating alternative forms of entrepreneurship that are sustainable, based on local products and services, and involve local people (Phillips et al., 2015). The design, development and operation of social enterprises require innovative thinking; thus, they may be considered social innovations themselves. Concepts approaching sustainable development, social policy, public services and economic well-being from the perspective of social innovation also emerged in the late 2000s (Weerakoon et al., 2016).

Let us now take a look at possible definitions of the concept itself.

According to Éva G. Fekete, a prominent researcher on the subject in Northern Hungary, since the regime change, micro-regional co-operations emerging as grassroots initiatives and involved in the implementation of regional innovations (G. Fekete, 2001) may also be considered social innovations. G. Fekete believes that one of the most important prerequisites for social innovations is being generated at a local, micro-level.

Howaldt et al. view social innovation as a new combination of social practices that can lead to a higher level of meeting social needs (Howaldt−Kopp−Schwarz, 2014). Terstriep and Rehfeld (2022) likewise highlight that social innovation is a novel combination of ideas and, as a new element, they also stress the importance of cooperation in generating these ideas among various social groups, that is, they describe it as a higher level of cooperation. Terstriep and Rehfeld add owing to interactions between groups, social innovations can contribute to reducing social inequalities and meet needs that cannot be met by the market. Similarly, Mulgan (2007) emphasises that social innovations provide solutions to unmet social needs.

Nemes and Varga offer an all-encompassing definition of social innovation: a process that may result in a new attitude, approach, paradigm, product, practice, process or network that deviates from previous practice and aims to solve problems and meet needs in society. Nemes and Varga point out that in the process, new attitudes, values, social relations and possibly new structures emerge (Nemes – Varga, 2015). Another vital element they highlight is that social innovations do not come from research institutions but are the result of the active role played by social and civil actors. Furthermore, they emphasise that social innovations are created in line with social norms and values, thus bearing in mind the reduction of environmental and social risks.

The European Commission defines social innovation as "new ideas (products, services and models) that simultaneously meet social needs (more effectively than alternatives) and create new social relationships or collaborations" (2013:39). In doing so, they can provide solutions to problems affecting social processes and ultimately improve the well-being of a region.

To summarise the above definitions, I shall discuss two ideas below. First, reviewing these theories, Hubert (2012) concludes that the concept of social innovation can be interpreted at three broad levels:

- Community level: the nature of innovation is described from the aspect of a grassroots initiative and as something that responds to unmet needs in the market and especially to the needs of vulnerable populations.
- Social level: innovation has an impact on the entire society, through the blurring of social and economic boundaries.

- Systemic level: involves changes in structures, strategies, policies and processes, through changes in attitudes and values.

Second, according to the Oslo Manual (2018), innovation emerges in knowledge, novelty, application and value creation.

Wigboldus (2016) describes 10 types of social innovation, based on the areas of emergence or application:

- legal innovation: innovation in legal frameworks
- cultural: innovation of non-formal institutions
- political: governmental, political innovations
- ideological: efforts to reform ideological frameworks
- ethical: a change in ethical and moral principles and the renewal of CSR activities of companies and firms
- economic: renewal and innovation in foreign trade and business
- organisational: potential for renewal in organisations
- technical: human and technological innovation, including social media
- ecological: interactions between people and the environment
- analytical: innovation of analytical and interpretative frameworks

During the implementation of social innovations several difficulties and obstacles may be encountered (Bogdány et al, 2023). Some of these derive from the fact that innovations fundamentally change the status quo, the usual way things are done, the widely used and often rigid patterns of action and thinking, and the way people relate to each other. Resistance to change is frequently experienced. Therefore, implementing innovations requires considering change management as a challenge.

On the other hand, often the necessary expertise is not available. A considerable proportion of social innovations is implemented in disadvantaged regions, among disadvantaged people. In such regions, it is often difficult to find suitably qualified and motivated people.

Thirdly, adequate financial conditions are often lacking, partly because of the circumstances mentioned above. If an innovation is implemented with grant funding, there is a common risk that it may not be sustained in the longer term after the project ends, precisely due to financial difficulties.

If these risks are not taken into account, we may run the risk of failure. Therefore, Bogdány et al. (2023) believe that social innovations can only be successfully implemented under the following boundary conditions:

- adequate human resources: support professionals who can initiate and facilitate processes, build a community and then equip the people involved with the knowledge necessary to ensure long-term sustainability
- a supportive business environment: a local community whose members can guarantee the success of the innovation by finding the right market for their own products and services, that is, by having sufficient demand
- innovation investments: external investors, creators and implementers of innovation
- collaborative networks, institutions: these provide the framework for successful innovation

Summarising this section, Figures 1 and 2 both offer a conclusion of and complement the above.

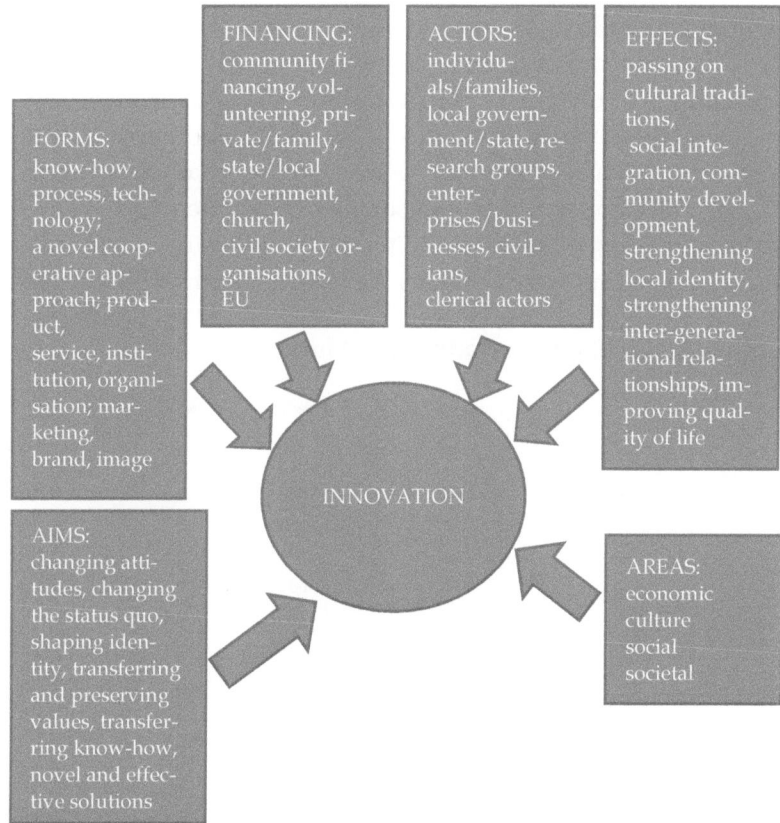

Figure 1: Summary model of social innovation
Source: own editing

Figure 1 summarises the main characteristic features of social innovation from six aspects.

First, in terms of the area they aim at, social innovations can be economic, cultural, social or societal — or a mixture of these.

Social innovations can be generated, that is, initiated and implemented by individuals, civil society organisations, research groups, churches, local government and state actors and business stakeholders. They can be aimed at changing attitudes or the status quo, preserving values, shaping identities, disseminating innovative and effective solutions and transferring know-how. The nature of the funding is important: social innovations can be financially supported by EU funds or by the state, local government, civil society organisations or churches. Funding may also be received from individuals, a community or a group, and it may come in the form of voluntary work (in addition to paid work). Medium- and long-term effects (obviously linked to the objectives) can include community development, improving quality of life, strengthening local identity, passing on cultural traditions, strengthening inter-generational relationships and achieving social inclusion more effectively.

Figure 2: Model for generating social innovation

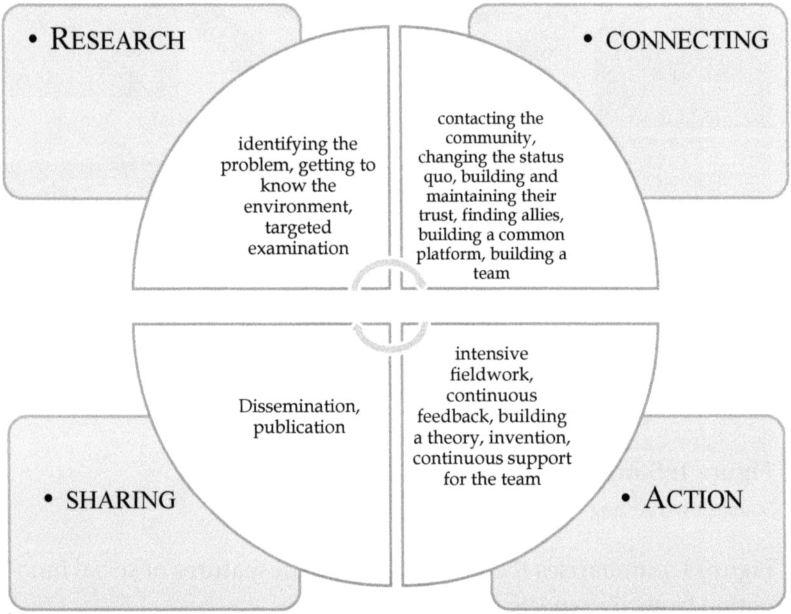

- RESEARCH: identifying the problem, getting to know the environment, targeted examination
- CONNECTING: contacting the community, changing the status quo, building and maintaining their trust, finding allies, building a common platform, building a team
- SHARING: Dissemination, publication
- ACTION: intensive fieldwork, continuous feedback, building a theory, invention, continuous support for the team

Source: own editing

Figure 2 illustrates the process by which social innovation is generated, implemented and then re-produced. It may start with thorough exploratory research, which involves identifying the problem or challenge and getting to know the context and the actors. In the second phase, the main element of which is connecting, the focus is on creating networks between actors, building and maintaining trust, developing collective reflection, creating a common platform and building a team. The third phase is one of intensive action and intervention, with continuous feedback, redesigning and providing support for the team. The final phase involves sharing the good experiences, risks and potential pitfalls with the wider public in order to complete the implementation of the innovation.

Measuring social innovation

A fascinating question related to social innovation is how to measure a community's or municipality's capacity to innovate, that is, all the capabilities and competencies that help generate and implement social innovations. This is generally known as innovation potential.

In this section, I present (a non-exhausting list of) models that aim to measure innovation potential. In Chapter 6.3, discussing case studies, I will also present a measurement tool we developed during an innovation project.

One of the most complex measurement methodologies was developed by the Economist Intelligence Unit at a national level in 2016. Their index measures the innovation potential of a country with a variety of indicators, both quantitative and qualitative, in the following four main dimensions:

- policy and institutional frameworks
- financing
- enterprises
- society

When developing the methodology, the researchers took into account the fact that a single system of indicators is not easy to establish. The geometric averages of the results measured along the four main dimensions are used to construct a complex social innovation index, which is standardised on a scale of 0-100. A specific process of weighing is also applied: policy and institutional frameworks (44.4%), financing (22.2%), enterprises (15%) and society (18.3%).

As mentioned earlier, a number of additional indicators are defined within each dimension. For example, the "society" pillar looks as follows:

Society:

- culture of volunteering
- political participation
- civil society activity
- trust in society
- freedom of the press

Looking at these indicators, it is clear to see that they are not easy to measure. How can one measure, for instance, a culture of volunteering or political participation? Thus, as the developers of the index claim, it is not possible to develop a single method of measurement, since the phenomenon to be measured is itself very complex and has diverse aspects.

Taking a different approach to the methodology, Castro Spila et al. (2016) do not measure innovation potential but its inverse, which they call vulnerability. The regional vulnerability index that they created is composed of four pillars: social, institutional, economic and environmental vulnerability.

The dimension of social vulnerability, for example, is measured using the following indicators:

- expenditure on health care (% of GDP)
- public expenditure on education (% of GDP)
- the total rate of "the vulnerable" employed (% of total) (e.g. unpaid family workers, self-employed)
  The indicators used for measuring institutional vulnerability are the following:
- public participation in government, freedom of the press
- government efficiency (quality of public services, bureaucracy)
- quality of regulations
- legal system
- control of corruption

In the framework of the TEPSIE project, Bund et al (2013) also developed a complex index to compare the innovation capacity of countries and regions. Their index measures in 3 dimensions and uses nearly 70 indicators:

- entrepreneurial activity pillar (dimensions: investment activity, start-up and closure rates, networking)
- theme-specific results pillar (dimensions: education, health, employment, housing, social capital and networks, political participation and environment),
- framework conditions pillar (dimensions: resources; social, political and institutional frameworks)

IndiSI—Indicators of Social Innovation is an improved version of TEPSIE. The design of the indiSI index is unique as it is divided into two phases: the first phase involves developing indicators and testing them through questionnaire research, while the second one draws on these results to refine them further through case studies of innovation actors.

Innovation is examined in the following seven areas, with themes identified within each area and indicators proposed for further measurement:

- education
- healthcare and care services
- employment
- housing
- social capital and network
- political participation
- environment

After the present review of the diverse theoretical literature on social innovations, the second chapter discusses the role of applied social sciences, including applied sociology, in generating and managing innovations.

References

Baturina, D.- Bezovan, G. (2015): *Social Innovation Impact-review*. Third Sector Impact Working Paper, Brussels. Microsoft Word—TSI_WP9 _Social Innovation-Final.docx (thirdsectorimpact.eu) (downloaded: 14/Sept/2024)

Bogdány E. – Máhr T. – Rentz T. – Rodek N.: *Bevezetés a társadalmi innovációba. Társadalmi innováció a közösségi jóllét szolgálatában.* [Introduction to Social Innovation – Social Innovation for Community Wellbeing]: https://mersz.hu/dokumentum/m1154bti__1/(download ed:20/Sept/2024)

Bund, E. – Hubrich, D. K. – Schmitz, B. – Mildenberger, G. – Krlev, G. (2013): *Blueprint of Social Innovation Metrics – Contributions to an Understanding of Opportunities and Challenges of Social Innovation Measurement. A Deliverable of the Project: "The Theoretical, Empirical and Policy Foundations for Building Social Innovation in Europe" (TEPSIE)*, European Commission, Brussels. (PDF) Blueprint of social innovation metrics: contributions to an understanding of opportunities and challenges of social innovation measurement (researchgate.net)

Castro Spila, J. – Luna, Á. – Unceta, A. (2016): *Social Innovation Regimes: An Exploratory Framework to Measure Social Innovation.* SIMPACT Working Paper, 2016 (1).

European Commission: Directorate General for Regional Policy: *Innovation in the National Strategic Reference Frameworks.* Brussels, 2006.

G. Fekete É. (2001): *Társadalmi innovációval a vidék fenntartható fejlődéséért* [Social innovation for Sustainable Rural Development]. TSZK tanulmanykotet.pdf (nemzetkozi-gazdalkodas.hu)

Howaldt, J – Kopp, R. – Schwarz, M. (2014): Zur Theorie sozialer Innovationen. Tardes vernachlässigter Beitrag zur Entwicklung einer soziologischen Innovationstheorie. Weinheim und Basel: Beltz Juventa.

Hubert, A. (2012): Foreword I. Challenge Social Innovation. In: J. H. J. H. Hans-Werner Franz (ed.): *Challenge Social Innovation: Potentials for Business, Social Entrepreneurship, Welfare and Civil Society.* Berlin/ Heidelberg: Springer.

INdSI https://www.soz.uni-heidelberg.de/indicators-of-social-innovation-indisi/

Mulgan, G. (2007): *Social Innovation: What It Is, Why It Matters and How Can Be Accelerated.* Skoll Centre for Social Entrepreneurship. Oxford Oxford: University, UK. https://youngfoundation.org/wp-content/uploads/2012/10/Social-Innovation-what-it-is-why-it-matters-how-it-can-be-accelerated-March-2007.pdf (downloaded:21/Oct./2024)

Nemes, G. – Varga, Á. (2015): *Társadalmi innováció és társadalmi tanulás a vidékfejlesztésben – sikerek, problémák, dilemmák* [Social Innovation and Social Learning in Rural Development – Successes, Challenges, Dilemmas]. In: „Mérleg és Kihívások" IX. Nemzetközi Tudományos Konferencia = "Balance and Challenges" IX. International Scientific Conference: A Gazdaságtudományi Kar megalapításának 25. évfordulója alkalmából [On the Occasion of the 25th Anniversary of the Establishment of the Faculty of Economics, University of Miskolc]. Miskolc: Miskolci Egyetem Gazdaságtudományi Kar, pp. 434-444. ISBN 978-963-358-098-1

Oslo Manual 2018: *Guidelines for Collecting, Reporting and Using Data on Innovation*, 4th Edition, The Measurement of Scientific, Technological and Innovation Activities, OECD Publishing, Paris/Eurostat, Luxembourg. Oslo Manual 2018 | OECD

Phillips, W. – Lee, H. – Ghobadian, A. – O'Regan, N. – James, P. (2015): Social Innovation and Social Entrepreneurship: A Systematic Review. *Group & Organization Management*, 40 (3): 428–461. https://doi.org/10.1177/1059601114560063

Schumpeter, J. (1934): *The Theory of Economic Development*. Cambridge: Harvard University Press.

Social innovation research in the European Union Approaches, findings and future directions Policy Review European Commission, 2013, 15. Social innovation research in the European Union – Publications Office of the EU (europa.eu)

Terstriep J – Rehfeld, D. 2022 The Economics of Social Innovation, Routledge: Taylor & Francic Group

Weerakoon, C. – McMurray, A. – Rametse, N. – Douglas, H. (2016): *Social innovation: a preliminary bibliometric analysis*. Social Innovation and Entrepreneurship Research Conference, Auckland, 10–12 February.

Seerp, W: Ten types of social innovation – a brief discussion paper https://edepot.wur.nl/407981 (downloaded: 23/Oct./2023)

Chapter 2
Applied Social Science Research and Social Innovation

Theory and application, research with a philanthropic approach and public policy intervention, "policy making" and scientific research, being a sociologist and social engineer — these terms have been well-known in this social science ever since its birth. It was Talcott Parsons, the 39th President of the American Sociological Association (1950), who first suggested finding the right balance between basic and applied research. was concerned with how sociologists could take the responsibility bestowed on them by the necessity of shaping society. He held the view that dealing with a problem systematically should be prioritised over finding an instant practical solution (Larson, 1995). In 1962 Paul Lazarsfeld, the 52nd president of ASA proposed "Sociology in Practice" or "Applied Sociology" for the title of the annual conference, thus signalling a need to reposition sociology. This act *per se* indicates the significance and recognition of the rise of applied sociology, at least in the USA. The conference addressed the crucial and increasingly indispensable issue of what challenges researchers face in translating practical problems into research questions and in turning research findings into proposals for action and social policies (Larson, 1995).

On applied sociology

In essence, applied sociology is the application of sociological theories, approaches and research methods to answer practical questions through shedding scientific light on, conducting research into and outlining possible solutions for social problems and concerns, in order to aid decision-makers, market participants and other actors in better understanding these issues. The role of the sociologist in the practical solution of a problem is another vital aspect. Sociologists may either keep their purely scientific role, that is, not participate in practical action — in this case the role of the scientist is separated from that of the intellectual activist — or they may blur the lines between the two. In the latter case (for instance in actionist sociology and sociological interventionism), sociology becomes applied and — departing the role of the scientist — the sociologist gets strongly involved in generating social processes and solving social problems.

The history of applied sociological research began more than 150 years ago, according to Lester F. Ward (Larson, 1995). For Ward, the task of applied sociology is to build a bridge between theory and practice, to bring sociological theories closer to social policy makers and to contribute to the development of sociological theories and methodology. Applied sociologists primarily aim to improve social life with the help of sociological theories and research, as well as by taking into account sociological standpoints and perspectives.

Similarly to Ward, some researchers believe that applied sociology is a continuation of the philanthropic approach that appeared and spread in the 19th century (Cf. Perlstadt, 2007; Larson, 1995). Others argue that the two developed separately: the latter emerged as a result of social problems and solutions among intellectuals and bourgeois circles sensitive to these issues, while the former was brought to life by universities, by researchers jointly and constantly fighting for the academic reputation of sociology (see Némedi, 1999/a; 1999/b; 2010).

In my view, the applied aspect of sociology may be traced back to its founder, Auguste Comte, who believed that one of the tasks of sociology was to gently guide public opinion and act as an advisor, that is, mediate between science and social activism. Comte made a distinction between social statistics and the science of social change, claiming that sociologists could indeed give advice but it was not their duty to participate in the practical implementation of the advice. As opposed to Comte, Herbert Spencer believed that sociologists did have the task of convincing the public and decision-makers that social processes should not be intervened with from outside but evolve spontaneously and naturally.

The term applied sociology was first used by Lester F. Ward (1883) (Larson, 1995), who believed that sociology had primacy over applied sociology, that is, the latter was dependent on "true," "pure" sociology. For Ward, sociology had the primary task of studying social principles and modes of operation, while stating in what direction and in what ways society could be developed came second. He claimed that applied sociology emerged from the original, "pure" sociology as a result of some evolutionary development (Ward, 2018).

Borrowing the term sociocrat from Comte, Ward believed that the government could improve society insofar as its decision-makers were well-versed in social sciences and that science-based legislation should be based on social statistics and sociology, as they have reliable sources to build social developments on. Yet, he was not in favour of radical social change coming from the left—he was convinced that success could only be achieved through education. He was of the opinion that the primary role of social science was to lay down the general principles that could serve as signposts for political and social action. He thus made a clear distinction between the role of the scientist and that of the activist: sociologists as scientists were not to get involved in solving any current social issues because that would make them politicians. He advocated value-free science. In contrast with Comte, Ward thought that the task of applied sociology was not to aid human communities in building an ideal society but to constructively contribute to the development of society and harmonise individual actions so that together they could contribute to the public good (Larson, 1995).

In order to support my research, in the following sections I shall provide a brief, and by no means exhaustive (since it would be impossible to discuss all efforts here), overview of the traditions of applied sociological research by mainly British, French, German and American social researchers and academics.

Along with the emergence and development of statistics (from 1800 to ca. 1880), the socio-political, philanthropic description of social problems appeared in England and France (Némedi, 1999/b). These descriptions and analyses were predominantly produced by physicians or well-intentioned non-professionals who, having come in contact with the lower sections of society, wished to better understand the social problems that affected these people. The rest of the descriptions were written by authors who regarded the victims of these negative processes as deviants and wanted to rehabilitate them. The latter studies were mainly based on moral statistics and, in Némedi's words, "driven by the desire for effective social control" (Némedi, 1999/b, p. 438). Their research was referred to as surveys, pointing to the original meaning of the word ('survey' as overview or research with qualitative elements). In England, these analyses were often prompted by the state setting up commissions of inquiry which examined important social issues and prepared reports based on interviews with the people concerned. Engels's *The Condition of the Working Class in England*, for example, was written on the basis of such reports.

In Great Britain in the 1830s and 1940s, amateur social researchers who applied statistical methods were members of the elite so they used their analyses and results directly for social reform. This period was the heyday of such surveys, with Manchester and then later London as its centre. Their decline was, in part, a result of the rise of social Darwinism and the improvement of living conditions.

The Charity Organization Society was founded in 1869 with the intent of helping the selection and separation of the "deserving poor" from other groups of poor people who were conditioned to live in poverty by state assistance and subsidies. As the society wished to base its support on scientific measurements and planned to provide practical assistance, it launched a training for social workers.

The above-mentioned socio-political debates informed Charles Booth's research on poverty in London as well. In addition to an extensive survey of poverty, Booth's goal was to examine the number of people living in primary poverty—a state developed due to lack of income—and of those living in poverty because of their lifestyle (Cf. Rowntree, 1971). Booth's research identified eight income categories and was published in eight volumes between 1889 and 1903. His research findings included the refutation of Malthus's thesis, and he empirically proved that the thesis of Social Darwinism that charity would increase poverty cannot be proved. He found that a considerable proportion of the poor are primary poor (that is, they have no sufficient income). Booth conducted interviews, studied minutes and statistical data, and made observations. A surprising finding of his research was that charity did not affect poverty levels; that is, it neither increased nor decreased poverty.

With regard to Great Britain, Némedi points out that the social sciences and sociological research that emerged at universities after World War II was part of the tradition outlined above and intertwined with it, albeit with some delay (Némedi, 1999/b).

Similarly, in France, (initially) non-professional social research related to social reforms appeared in the mid-1800s. Physician Louis R. Villermé carried out a six-year-long research among textile factory workers, systematically describing the work processes and the situation of the workers (including women and children), as well as the hygiene conditions of work.

A more well-known researcher, Frédéric Le Play wrote family monographs, thoroughly describing the budget, history, lifestyle and working conditions of families. His goal was to detect and restore social peace and harmony; that is, to find the reasons at the core of people's happiness. He used two concepts still fundamental in debates in social policy today—freedom and security –, and claimed that security was more of a priority. He produced a family typology and suggested that the stability of the family could be increased by a move towards family ties, towards a patriarchal family. Le Play had an impact on English social scientists as well, and worked on institutionalising the paternalistic, conservative, reform-based social science he advocated (Botos, 1996).

In an overview of the role of French social researchers, Émile Durkheim's oeuvre needs to be highlighted. His 1897 work *Suicide* was the first major sociological work that can be regarded as a combination of theoretical work (following the tradition of Comte) and practical social research (Quetelet's moral statistics). Yet, as Némedi argues (Némedi, 1999/b), this work cannot be considered a continuation of problem-oriented empirical social research.

Within the French tradition of applied sociology, Alaine Touraine's actionalist sociology must also be mentioned. In developing his theory, Touraine studied the emergence and development of social movements (Pokol, 1995). He strove to develop a more up-to-date, more modernised form of Marxist social theory, incorporated structuralist and functionalist theories and put an emphasis on the analysis of social conflict. He believed that the former explained how social order was maintained, while the latter could capture the dynamic nature of society, how change and the groups of power that propel it function. Touraine's study of social movements led to the findings that these movements were the driving force behind social change. From the 1970s on, Touraine's attention increasingly shifted to sociological interventionism. He believed that the role of the sociologist was to bring together the organisers of social movements, and thus help elevate them to a more conscious level. Having formulated his theory, Touraine himself turned towards practice and continued his career as a "policy-maker."

In Germany, the Verein für Socialpolitik (The Association for Social Policy) was founded in 1872 and discussed social and economic issues right from the start. The association aimed at developing economics with ethical considerations rather than an independent social science. As Némedi points out, although Max Weber, too, was involved in the research carried out by the association (along with Tönnies, Alfred Weber and Sombart), the issues explored there were not featured in his theoretical work, which means that sociological theory and the social sciences research discussed above were not interlinked in Germany either (Némedi, 2010).

In the USA, moral social reformers did not have the same political influence as reformers in Great Britain. Thus, the former turned to local communities and later to universities in their research on social phenomena, as a result of which considerable empirical social research was carried out even before sociology emerged at universities. Statistical research on public health was first conducted in the United States in the late 1980s (Perlstadt, 2007).

Empirical social research grew out of poverty research and was interlaced with European settlement-type social assistance. In the 1890s, activists of Hull House settlement in Chicago (Kelley, Addams and others, joined by researchers John Dewey and George

Herbert Mead) were convinced that thoroughly documenting the living conditions of the poor could help start vital social reforms. In those years, drawing on Charles Booth's research in London, the staff members systematically mapped the neighbourhood and prepared in-depth descriptions of the inhabitants. The activists believed that practice and the knowledge gained from it were more important than theory.

Modelled on Toynbee Hall in East London, Hull House was founded in 1884 with the primary goal of aiding working-class people's access to education and improving social assistance. In 1892, Addams published "The Three Rs" of settlement work (Residence, Research, and Reform), which were the core elements of the mission of Hull House: cooperation with the locals, intensive research into their living conditions (poverty, dependency), continuously informing the public and urging societal and social reform (Hilscher, 1989).

In *The Negro in Philadelphia* (1899), W.E.B. DuBois, the first black social scientist, carried out research on the black neighbourhoods of Philadelphia. One of his aims was to demonstrate that blacks were not a homogeneous group but that had middle-class individuals among them. Although DuBois could not find a job at a good university after publishing his work and thus later became a journalist, he was an employee of the University of Philadelphia at the time of the research, so it can be regarded as university research (Némedi, 1999/b).

The Pittsburgh Survey (1906-1909) was a sociological project involving the collaboration of social workers and university researchers in order to facilitate the goals of urban reformers (The Pittsburgh District, 1914). It was such a success that it led to a survey movement in the USA: a unique combination of academic research, journalism and social engineering, prevalent until the 1930s. A survey required the work of three types of professionals: social researchers, who would explore the situation, social planners, who would contribute to social reforms with their proposals and socalled "disseminators," carrying out the widespread dissemination of the necessary proposals and educating the public to make them as receptive as possible.

Ernest Burgess, a professor at the University of Chicago, had reservations about this survey research and criticised its methodology (which might be interpreted as defending the hard-won scientific reputation of sociology as an academic discipline).

At this time, university researchers relied on ethnographic observations and personal documents in addition to statistics and only started to use the survey method later, after the decline of the original survey movement (Feischmidt, 2006).

The report "Recent Social Trends in the United States" was produced in 1933, with the intention to demonstrate that empirical sociology was an independent academic field, rather than a continuation of 19th-century empirical social research.

One good example of applied sociology used outside the academia is the factory of the Ford Motor Company: in the early 1910s, Henry Ford had the idea to set up a sociology department to observe, research and select workers for a special programme (the programme and its humanity were criticised by many and from many aspects).

In 1929, William F. Ogburn proclaimed that sociology as a scientific field was not competent to make the world a better place (Perlstadt, 2007). Yet, he believed that applied research was based on scientific methods and that these should be separated from propaganda, ethics, religion and journalism. He advocated for drawing a sharp contrast between "policy making" and scientific research. Ogburn distinguished between sociologists and social engineers: the former being research scientists and the latter as practitioners applying certain methods and knowledge in practice but not scientists (Larson, 1995).

The Office of Facts and Figures was set up in the USA during World War II for the purpose of opinion polling in areas related to the war (e.g. public opinion on the war and the restrictions imposed). When examining the background of applied sociological research, Robert K. Merton and Paul F. Lazarsfeld should also be mentioned briefly. Merton and Lazarsfeld advocated the development of the middle-range theory and co-founded the Centre for Applied Social Research. Among other scholarly endeavours, Merton contributed greatly to the development of the methodology of empirical sociology and is known for developing the methodology of focus group interviews.

Rensis Likert, a social psychologist, researcher and creator of the Likert scale, who significantly facilitated the practical application of the findings of behavioural science, conducted a study with his peers after World War II which could then be utilised by the financial world, organisations, governmental and other customers.

As discussed earlier, in 1950 Talcott Parsons, as the 39th President of the American Sociological Association suggested finding the appropriate balance between basic and applied research. In the 1960s, several university-affiliated institutes for social research were founded in the USA. Their research made a significant contribution to the development of sociological theories and to methodological renewal (e.g. possibilities of the widespread use of case studies). As an ASA President, Paul Lazarsfeld likewise played a vital role in separating applied sociology from "pure sociology."

In the late 1970s and early 1980s, many students earned a master's or PhD degree in sociology but US higher education had limitations in accommodating university professors. Thus, many of the latter found work outside the academia, thereby increasing the size of the social scientific research community and raising the profile of the approach. The present situation in Hungary is quite similar.

By the mid-20th century (in almost all the countries studied above), non-professional but highly enthusiastic reformers were replaced by professional researchers and scholars. Later, market researchers and opinion pollsters increasingly emerged as members of professional market undertakings, which made no such efforts as 19th-century social reformers.

The issue of basic research versus applied research appears regularly (and increasingly) among scholars of sociology and social sciences (as well as in scientific policy). In light of the above, it is my belief that the task of applied sociology in the 21st century is to act as a mediator between theory and practice (in the spirit of the work of Ward and others), incorporating elements of sociology that may be utilised socially.

The epistemological background of applied social sciences (including sociology)

While positivism is built on determinisms (causality and determination), hermeneutics promotes indeterminism, the freedom of human will and behaviour: it believes that human behaviour is impacted by feelings, impressions and beliefs (as well) (Feischmidt, 2006; Larson, 1995; Kvale, 2005; Mason, 2001). In hermeneutics, an interpretative understanding of actions is of core importance. Its basic principle is that the study of human behaviour can never be complex and exact since it is always already characterised by uncertainties. In addition, it may be inferred that sociological factors never exist on their own but are in constant flux and are thus difficult to measure. From a hermeneutic aspect, it is vital to look for causality and subjective meaning behind actions and social events (Denzin and Lincoln, 2011).

In contrast with positivism, Lincoln and Guba's naturalistic approach (Lincoln and Guba, 1985; 1982) asserts that there exist multiple realities, that the cogniser and the object of cognition are not inseparable but constantly interact, that it is not possible to draw a clear distinction between causality and consequences as everything is interconnected and in constant change, and that cognition is in fact always value-filled. Lincoln and Guba use the approach of continuous theory construction, with multiple, even overlapping, constantly changing working hypotheses (these ideas form the basis of a major part of qualitative research, see also Glaser and Strauss, 1967; Bryman, 2015; Feischmidt, 2006). Guba and Lincoln insert an approach of interdeterminism into sociological practice: they claim that generalisations and final conclusions made by researchers are basically constructions of the human mind, not something that exist in an inherent, exact way. This means that all truth is relative, all statements are dependent on context and there are no universally valid, definitive findings. Therefore, how results found in one place, in one context, can be transported to another is a crucial question. Does it work in other places, in other circumstances? The solution Lincoln and Guba propose is fit and congruence, that is, describing the similarities and differences between the two cases. What follows is that they reject constructing theory in a deductive, axiomatic way (as well as any approach building on the methodology of grounded theory).

Ralf Bohnsack (cited in Feischmidt, 2006) discusses knowledge embedded in position, meaning that researchers are part of the 'reality' they observe, so reality does not exist independently of them. Bohnsack draws on the phenomenological view that social facts do not exist on their own so the researchers' interpretations are only secondary constructions.

The model (and approaches) outlined above may provide the base for applied research that is particular, bound by time and place, can form the basis of planning processes, and serve the purpose of constructing theories and generating explanations based on in the sense that it does not deny the important role the observer plays in the process of interpretation so it is (more) suitable as a background for value-filled socio-political decisions (as well) than positivist paradigms. I believe that applied social sciences should have such a hermeneutic, interpretative approach.

Applied social science research and social innovation

Throughout my applied social science research, I have increasingly found that the problem-solving model developed in social casework, the research methodology model commonly applied to sociological research and the model I have developed in generating social innovations indeed correspond to each other and can thus be used complementarily in practice (see Figures 1-3).

Sometimes the process reaches the stage of an in-depth exploration of the problem, other times we get to the point where we can offer solutions and make social policy proposals, and in some cases, we end up generating processes for social change (either in the spirit of actionist sociology or by generating social innovations). Sociological research can have a cathartic or therapeutic character on its own, although the application of therapeutic or psychological aspects is not part of purely sociological work per se. Still, as an unintended impact, even research on a group, organisation or community can have a revelational effect and character (not to mention life history or other exploratory interviews, which almost inevitably trigger similar responses—for more on this, see Kvale, 2005; Mason, 2001).

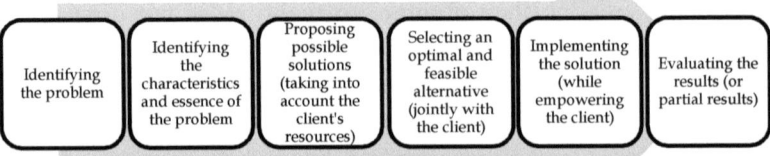

Figure 1: The problem-solving model of social work
Source: own design

The problem-solving model applied in social casework was originally developed by Helen Harris Perlman (Perlman, 1957), who was active in the field of applied social sciences as a social worker, researcher and teacher for nearly seventy years. Pioneering the Chicago School of social service practice, Perlman published her seminal *Social Casework: the Problem Solving Process* (1957), which has been the basis for the problem-solving approach of social work ever since.

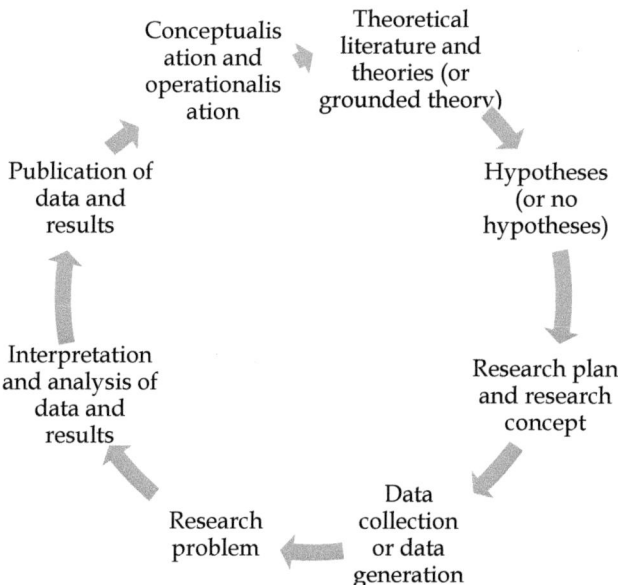

Figure 2: Steps of sociological research (a general model)
Source: own design

Figure 2 illustrates a well-known model for sociological research. In the basic model, each phase of the research work is presented as one step but in reality these phases are more like decisions to be made parallelly — often momentary decisions, for instance in the case of applying grounded theory. As opposed to the positivist approach, qualitative research often follows an inductive logic. Here, data generation (rather than data collection) is more prevalent (Mason, 2001) due to the epistemological starting point mentioned above (the researcher is part of 'reality') and it also involves active and retroactive processes that can be adjusted flexibly.

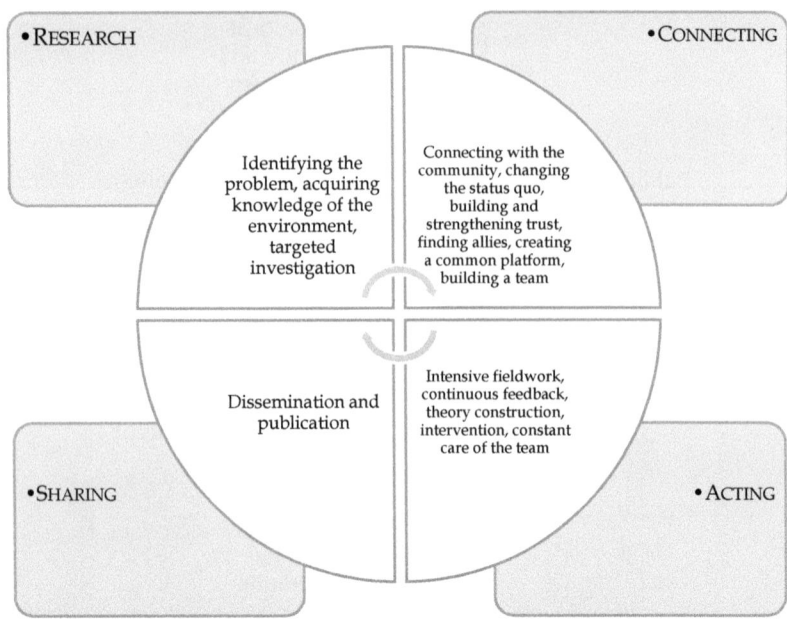

Figure 3: The model of generating social innovations
Source: own design

Finally, the model of generating social innovation (Figure 3), described in detail in the previous chapter, illustrates the process by which social innovations are developed and implemented. Vital elements of this process include in-depth exploration, acquiring knowledge of the environment of the innovation, identifying the stakeholders of the innovation, gaining their trust, involving them in the processes (all these are equally present in action research), intensive presence in fieldwork, as well as monitoring, facilitating and disseminating processes, and even the continuous development of a kind of grounded theory with a scientific interest.

References

Botos M. (1996): Frederic Le Play. *Magyar Szemle*, 5 (5):516-529.

Bryman, A. (2015): *Social Research Methods*. Oxford: Oxford University Press.

Denzin, N. K. – Lincoln, I. S. (2011): *The SAGE Handbook of Qualitative Research*. London: Sage Handbooks, Sage.

Feischmidt M. (2006): *A kvalitatív módszerek története.* [History of Qualitative Methods.] http://mmi.elte.hu/szabadbolcseszet/mmi.elte.hu/szabadbolcseszet/index6f90.html?option=com_tanelem&id_tanelem=830&tip=0 (downloaded:14/Sept/2024)

Glaser, B. G.—Strauss, A. I. (1967): *The Discovery of Grounded Theory Strategies for Qualitative Research.* A Division of Transaction Publishers New Brunswick (U.S.A.) and London (U.K.): AldineTransaction.

Guba, E. G.—Lincoln, Y. S (1985): *Naturalistic Inquiry.* London: Sage Publications.

Guba, E. G.—Lincoln, Y. S (1982): Naturalistic Inquiry. *Educational Technology Research and Development ECTJ,* 30, (4):233-252.

Hilscher R. (1989): A Settlement-mozgalom. [The Settlement Movement.] *Esély,* (1):55-64.

Kvale, S. (2005): *Az interjú – Bevezetés a kvalitatív kutatás interjútechnikáiba.* [The interview – An introduction to interview techniques for qualitative research.] Budapest: Jószöveg Kiadó.

Mason, J. (2001): *Qualitative Researching.* London: Sage Publications.

Némedi D. (1999/a): Auguste Comte: A szociológia megalapítója? [Auguste Comte: The Founder of Sociology?] In Felkai G. (szerk.): *A szociológia kialakulása.* Budapest: Új Mandátum Kiadó.

Némedi D. (1999/b): Empirikus társadalomkutatás a tizenkilencedik század végéig. [Empirical Social Research until the End of the Nineteenth Century.] In Felkai G. (szerk.): *A szociológia kialakulása.* Budapest: Új Mandátum Kiadó.

Némedi D. (2000): A szociológia egy sikeres évszázad után. [Sociology After a Successful Century.] *Szociológiai Szemle,* (2):3-16.

Némedi D. (2010): Bevezetés: a szociológia problémája – ma. [Introduction: the Problem of Sociology – Today.] In Némedi D. (szerk.): *Modern szociológiai paradigmák.* Budapest: Napvilág Kiadó, második kiadás.

Larson, C. J. (1995): Theory and Applied Sociology. *Journal of Applied Sociology,* 12 (2):13-29.

Perlman, H. H. (1957): *Social Casework: A Problem-solving Process.* Chicago: University of Chicago Press.

Perlstadt, H. (2007): Applied Sociology. In Bryant, C. D.—Peck, D. L. (szerk.): *21st Century Sociology.* London: Sage Publications.

Pokol B. (1995): *Modern francia szociológiaelméletek.* [Modern French Sociological Theories.] Miskolc: Bíbor Kiadó.

Chapter 3
Design Thinking, "Wicked" Problems and Social Innovation: From Theory to Practice

As discussed in the introduction to this book, since the late 20th century, humanity has faced several challenges that make us feel increasingly vulnerable. In Risk Society: Towards a New Modernity, Ulrich Beck implies that modernity is concomitant with globally emerging risks that increase our sense of vulnerability and uncertainty (Beck, 2006). These challenges are not time- and space-specific, and are difficult to decipher and be linked to issues of causality and responsibility.

The question thus arises: can postmodern society be described as being in a permanent state of crisis? Paul Reitter and Chad Wellmon (Reitter and Wellmon, 2021) argue that the entire history of humanity may be regarded as a history of a search for meaning; that is, attempts to fill the uncertain and fragile human condition with what is believed to be certain. From this viewpoint, human existence does appear to be a continuous struggle between 'nothing' and 'something.' The question that follows is how we cope with this at the level of the individual, the community and society. What problem-solving strategies do we have available to resolve critical situations and crises? Elemér Hankiss and Mária Kopp have found that Hungarian society can be described by a state of learned helplessness (Kopp, 2008; Hankiss, 1980), meaning that the Hungarian public spirit characteristically trivializes and neglects problems instead of finding solutions: they tend not to give a substantive reply, their reaction is not proactive but (at best) reactive, and they only react when they absolutely have to. Instead of this quite visceral solution, Hankiss and Kopp recommend relying on learned talent. As Hankiss explains in many of his writings and interviews, learned talent means that we stop complaining and are resourceful in solving a critical situation.

How can we be resourceful? How can we respond to crisis and uncertainty proactively? With the help of the coping strategies discussed by Erikson (1965), Caplan (Oláh, 2021) and Lazarus and Folkman (1988), and described as adaptive coping skills.

How is all this related to design thinking, "wicked" problems and social innovation? Horst W. J. Rittel and Melvin M. Webber's "Dilemmas in General Theory of Planning" (1973) provides a powerful lesson for designing social processes. The study makes a distinction between so-called tame and wicked problems: the former are well structured and solvable, while the latter are not well structured and there is not one good solution to them, as often it is not known what the real problem is or how it could be made tangible. Rittel and Webber assert that most societal challenges are "wild" or "wicked" problems. And what can be done about such problems — problems that are hard to define and there is not one good solution to? Applying design thinking can provide a range of alternative, potentially good solutions. Furthermore, placing the whole process at the service of social and community design, design thinking can be combined with innovative, original solutions leading us to social innovation. Design thinking, challenges posed by wicked problems and social innovations have several things in common. At their core they are characterised by divergence and seeking alternatives rather than one optimal solution, as well as by human-centred design, considering the needs of the users (which may be a local community or a group, which means community design), a specific empathic approach and, finally, solution focus and creativity.

In the following sections, I shall highlight the interrelationships of these three concepts. The significance of the chapter lies in connecting design thinking to the processes of generating social innovations, as discussed in the previous chapters: it offers a selection of design methods I have complied from the methodologies of coaching, community design, design thinking and community design. In addition, the chapter takes account of the aspects of how changes at the micro (individual), meso (community or group) and macro levels may be facilitated, which means that the methods presented here can be suitable to initiate change at all three levels.

Thinking and design thinking

Thinking is the highest level of cognition. In behaviourist theory, thinking is in fact behaviour itself. It is a function enabling humans to talk, learn concepts, set rules, solve problems and draw conclusions.

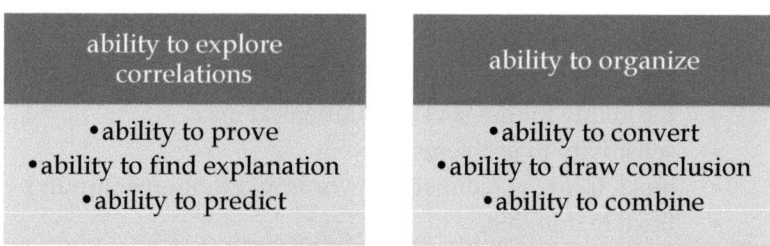

Figure 1: Components of thinking
Source:http://www.staff.u-szeged.hu/~nagyjozs/prof.emeritus.OLD/pdf/28_a_ gondolkodasi_kulcskompetencia_fejlodessegitese(229-236).pdf, p. 231.

As shown in Figure 1, thinking happens on the basis of eight different cognitive abilities: four interpretive (above domains) and four experiential (below domains) abilities.

Thinking has three functions:

- association: connecting thoughts, images and experiences (without a goal)
- problem-solving: exploring the essence and interrelationships of things, clarifying the meaning and relationships of things already known, knowing knowledge
- understanding: discovering the essence of things and their interrelationships

Thinking can be convergent or divergent. In the case of convergent thinking, we move towards a solution in logical steps. This method can be used to solve tame problems. Divergent or discontinuous thinking, on the other hand, is heuristic: it offers multiple alternatives and there may not be a single good solution to the problem. As demonstrated earlier, divergent thinking can be an efficient method for dealing with wicked problems.

In an article published in 1950, Joy Paul Guilford actually writes about divergent thinking and design thinking when defining creativity as creative power, the ability to create, in which diverse faculties together enable combining isolated experiences, interpreting them in novel ways and expressing them in new forms (Guilford, 1950). Characteristics of a creative mind include:

- divergent thinking,
- the ability to see something from multiple perspectives,
- the ability to find several solutions at once,
- sensitivity to problems,
- quick thinking (connecting words and thoughts rapidly),
- flexible thinking,
- originality of thinking (unusual solutions),
- striving for change,
- boldness, impulsiveness and openness,
- nonconformism and questioning authority,
- reacting to new situations quickly, flexibly and spontaneously.

Since the 1960s, design thinking has gained ground in areas and circles utterly different from the design profession itself. In the 1980s and 1990s, design thinking spread to business, the field of organisational culture, and was increasingly present in the activities of organisations and communities identifying themselves as so-called "learning organisations."

Peter G. Rowe's book Design Thinking, published by Cambridge Publishing in 1987, demonstrated how the method could be used in the fields of architecture and urban planning. Then IDEO was founded in 1991– an organisation that built a model for the widespread use of design thinking. In his 1982 article "Designerly Ways of Knowing," Nigel Cross points out that everything we see around us has had to be designed. He argues that science, art and design all contribute to developing our cognitive capacities. Science helps us by finding similarities between things that are seemingly different (e.g. creating models and establishing laws), art distinguishes between seemingly identical things (such as a particular way of representing the same thing in different ways), and design makes previously invisible things visible, that is, it gives them a shape and form.

This means that design thinking is both an agile tool and a way of thinking. It is a creative problem-solving process that takes a proactive stance in response to needs generated by the socio-economic environment—it finds innovative solutions. Constant connection with users and a strong focus on solutions are core elements. Design thinking can be a useful tool in our private lives and for life design. It is frequently used in coaching and consulting processes, as it is a highly effective and innovative method for redefining problems, finding new approaches, and developing creative solutions and alternatives. Design thinking can be particularly effective when there are no usual solutions or when usual solutions fail.

The four principles of design thinking are the following:

- "The human rule.": Design activities are all social and human-centred, that is, they involve a human being.
- "The ambiguity rule": Ambiguity and questioning are unavoidable as the "product" takes shape through continuous development.
- "All design is redesign": Social circumstances may change but human needs do not.
- "The tangibility rule": Design thinking involves ongoing dialogue with the users and feedback can only be given if there is a "product" to discuss.[1]

Design thinking and wicked problems

Design thinking is all about experimentation: it necessarily involves discarding the usual solution and exploring as many different solutions as possible. So it's. As mentioned earlier, it is especially suitable for solving "wicked problems," particularly challenging issues.

---

[1] What Exactly Is Design Thinking? [Updated Guide for 2023] (careerfoundry.com) https://careerfoundry.com/en/blog/ux-design/what-is-design-thin king-everything-you-need-to-know-to-get-started/#what-is-design-thinking

The concept of "wicked problem" was first discussed in a 1973 article by Rittel and Weber. The authors differentiate between so-called tame problems, which are generally well structured and have an optimal solution, and wicked problems, which are the exact opposite (Rittel—Weber, 1973). Understanding wicked problems is like oscillation—thinking about them is a perpetual process that cannot be completed, only stopped at a certain point. As traditional methods are unsuitable for dealing with persistent, complex, wicked problems, it is worth utilising design thinking.

Stages of design thinking

Stanford d.school illustrates the five stages of the design thinking process in the following model:

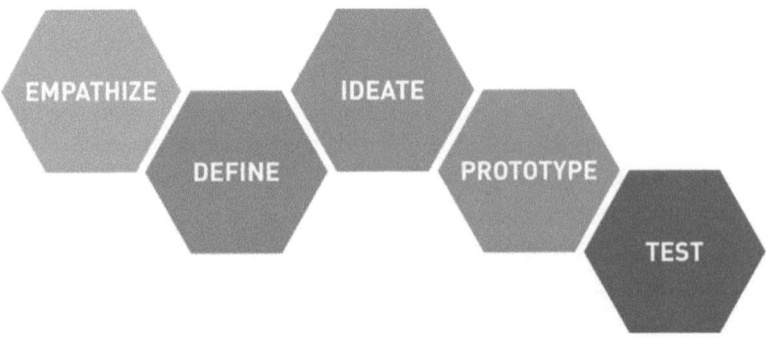

Figure 2: Stages of the design thinking process
Source: https://dschool.stanford.edu

„Stage 1. Emphasise: Seeking to understand the background of the phenomenon non-judgmentally and as fully as possible and exploring the problem in its broadest sense.

Stage 2. Define: Defining the personas, the subject, the objective, the risks and threats, and the challenge per se.

Stage 3. Ideate: Sharing all ideas, solutions and alternatives without judgement, using "yes and" thinking and then prioritising.

Stage 4. Prototype: Materialising the most suitable ideas. These prototypes or "products" can be almost anything: a written work, a model, or an activity. Solution-focused design is paramount, so this phase allows for making mistakes and learning from them.

Stage 5. Test: Getting feedback on the prototype to facilitate improvement and thus to meet the needs of the users. Stanford d.school's advice is "always prototype as if you know you're right, but test as if you know you're wrong."[2]

The entire process can be repeated, if needed, over and over again, iteratively.

Social innovations and design thinking

As pointed out in Chapter 1, as opposed to technological innovations, social innovations characteristically focus on renewing human potential, they are made in simple workshops instead of in advanced research laboratories, their theory is shaped by practical experience and they require widespread public cooperation. Social innovations respond primarily to societal challenges such as dealing with territorial disparities, promoting social inclusion, improving the quality of people's lives in a region, strengthening local identity, enhancing creative problem-solving, developing communities, and facilitating intergenerational resource flows and connections.

Social innovation is strongly correlated with design thinking. Both can be applied to the five phases already described above (understanding the background of the phenomenon or the cause, defining the challenge, brainstorming, prototyping and testing). By linking the two, the following section will present some design methods that can be used effectively in both design thinking and making social innovations, as well as in individual or community coaching, especially for "wicked" problems, which require divergent thinking.

Emphasising: identifying and exploring a problem

Design thinking is effective primarily in the case of unusual, "wicked" and complex problems and challenges, which tend to be

---

[2] https://web.stanford.edu/~mshanks/MichaelShanks/files/509554.pdf

hard to dissect, that is, it is difficult to understand them as a series of logical, linear steps, to explore what lies in their background and to map the correlations.

The problem tree and objective tree methods are frequently used in designing social projects, as they both illustrate this complexity above and help structure thinking. They are also useful for identifying which area a certain challenge addresses and which one the design offers solutions to.

Effects of the problem

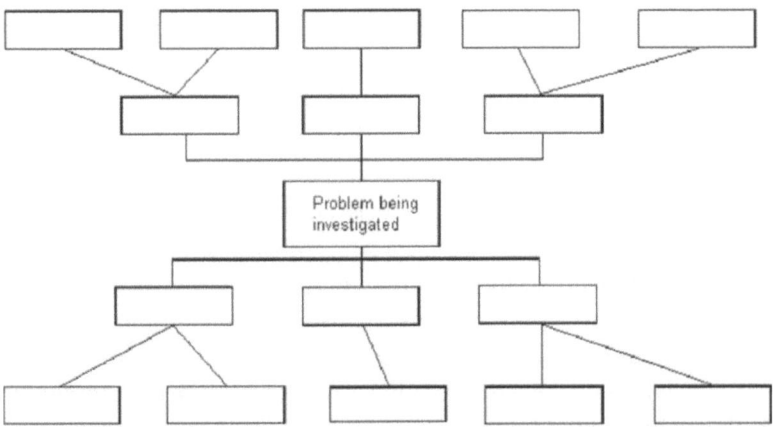

Causes of the problem

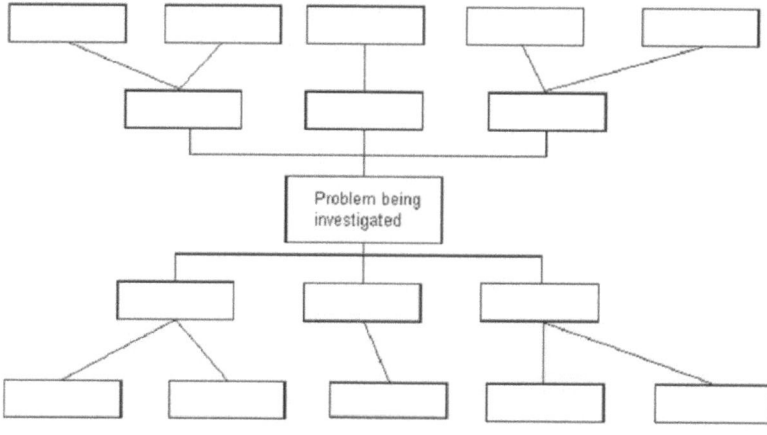

Figure 3: Problem tree and solution tree

Source: https://www.researchgate.net/publication/23262328_Problem_and_soluti on_trees_A_practical_approach_for_identifying_potential_interventions_to_impro ve_population_nutrition/download?_tp=eyJjb250ZXh0Ijp7ImZpcnN0UGFnZSI6Il 9kaXJlY3QiLCJwYWdlIjoiX2RpcmVjdCJ9fQ

In the problem tree method, we start with the main problem or challenge, then search for its primary and secondary causes, and finally get to the root of the problem. Likewise, the objective tree is prepared analogically, but here problems are turned into objectives.

Another useful method for identifying a challenge is the random word technique, which improves associative thinking skills.

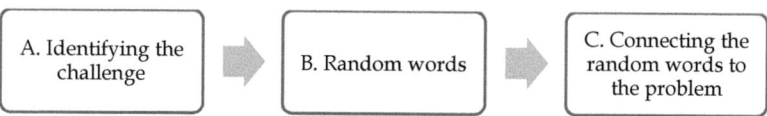

Figure 4: The random word technique

Source: own editing

To clearly identify an emerging challenge, we connect it to randomly "found" words or concepts. For instance, we can randomly select ten words from a written text or write down the first ten words that come to mind and then look for ways of associating each of them with the problem to be solved, thereby improving our associative skills and creativity. We can and do the same. By the end, it will be clear to see that we can associate almost anything with almost anything.

A third possible tool is creating a mind map, a well-known method used for brainstorming.

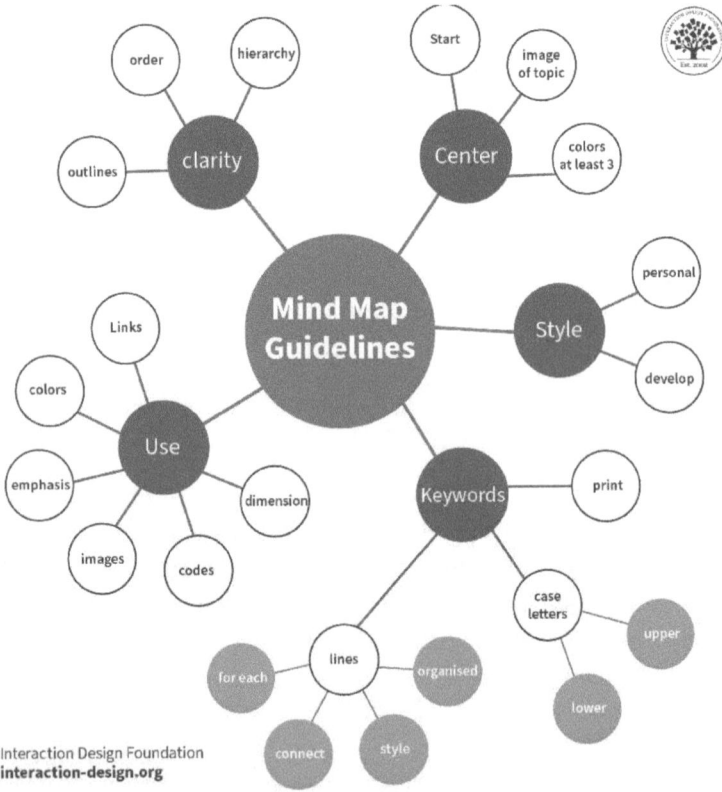

Figure 5: The mind map method
Source: Interaction Desing Foundation
https://www.interaction-design.org/literature/topics/mind-maps

Mind mapping starts with writing down a certain challenge and then everything that comes to mind in connection with it, which helps bring to light various aspects of the phenomenon or any related factors. Through visualising and "exhibiting," the mind map can be used to increase the visibility of the problem and organise our thoughts about it.

The fourth method is adaptive reasoning – frequently used in marketing – which aims to personalise the challenge, problem, "product," service to be developed or the target group to develop for. It may also be referred to as an empathy map since personalising gives the phenomenon a personal touch.

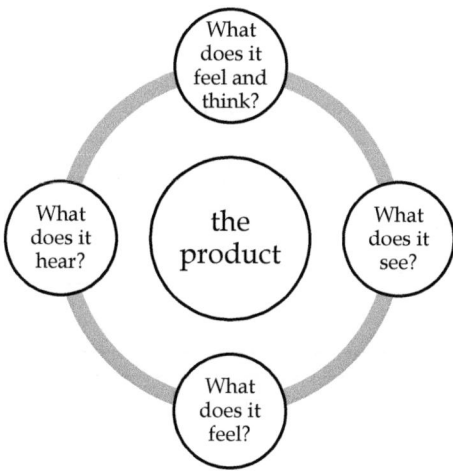

Figure 6: Adaptive reasoning
Source: own editing

If, for instance, our goal is to improve disadvantaged children's quality of life through a social innovation project, adaptive reasoning can facilitate specifying what to improve and how. Let us consider the four questions presented in Figure 6: What could these children possibly think and feel? What do they see around them? What do they hear? What do they say and do? Contemplating these questions will help us design a more effective and complex service for or related to these disadvantaged children. Furthermore, the method complies with the criterion of both design thinking and social innovation ideas: the individual or, in other words, the user's needs are the starting point.

Define: Clearly defining the challenge and setting objectives

The problem tree and the objective tree methods have been described in detail above. Once the challenge has been clearly defined and other factors and their relationship have been clarified, the goal tree can help us determine the project objectives and their aspects.

At this stage, three-point estimating is another possible method.

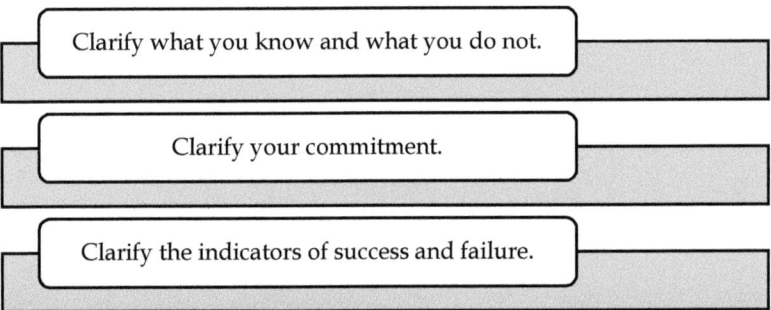

Figure 7: Three-point estimating
Source: own editing

The significance of the three points lies in enabling a clear understanding of the available information, the information still needed, and where it could be obtained from. It also facilitates considering how much interest we have in the implementation of the project, and how committed and motivated we are to carry it out. With the help of this method, potential risks and threats can be collected and compared with our prospects of success, and we can clarify what may be regarded as successful implementation.

Ideate: Brainstorming for possible solutions and alternatives

Once we know exactly what to design and what objectives to achieve, we can move on to elaborating possible paths, solutions and alternatives.

One excellent way of fine-tuning ideas is the so-called Scamper method, originally developed by Alex Osborn in the 1950s and further developed by Bob Eberle in his 1996 book (Eberle, 1966).

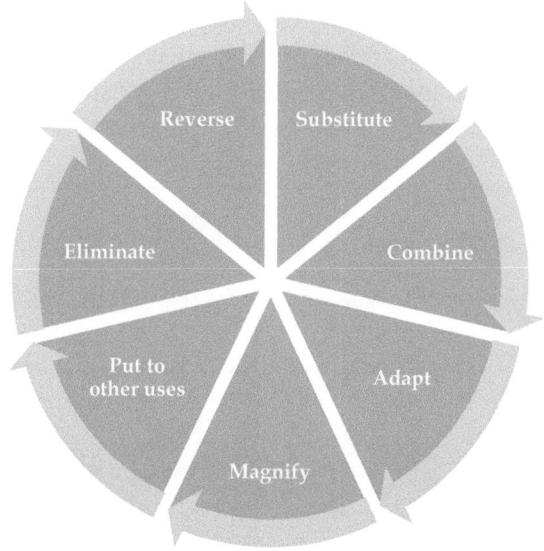

Figure 8: The SCAMPER technique
Source: own editing

The process involves considering seven aspects in order to get closer to finding all the possible solutions and to carefully consider the service (product, know-how, etc.) to be developed, by answering the following questions:

- Substitute: Who to substitute with? What to substitute with? Another raw material? Something else?
- Combine: Combine with what? Jointly? Combined ideas? Combined forces?
- Adapt: What other ideas are there? What does it refer to? What can be adapted? What could be used for it?
- Magnify: What else could be added?
- Put to other uses: What else could it be used for? What alternatives are there?

53

- Eliminate: Which element/Who should be removed from it?
- Reverse: Should it be reversed, done in a different order? Exchange something? Change rhythm?

"Six Thinking Hats," developed by psychologist Edward de Bono is another useful method. Well-known and applied in several fields, the method involves parallel thinking, listening to and considering one other's (different) vantage points and arguments.

Figure 9: The Six Thinking Hats method
Source: https://readingraphics.com/book-summary-six-thinking-hats/

The method can also be used alone, by one person who puts the different coloured hats on and thinks about the challenge from different perspectives. It is also a great way for brainstorming in a group (it was originally developed for this purpose), where each actor represents a different perspective or point of view, or the leader puts on different hats or all group members wear the same hat at a given stage. Either way, the discussion starts and ends wearing the blue hat, thus creating the framework for brainstorming. The white hat represents facts and the red one represents feelings. The green hat stands for ideas and creativity, the black one for objections and the yellow one for positivity, emphasising the advantages.

The third method is the so-called "Imaginary Friends" technique. Similarly to "Six Thinking Hats," it serves the purpose of collectively presenting different points of view and ways of thinking.

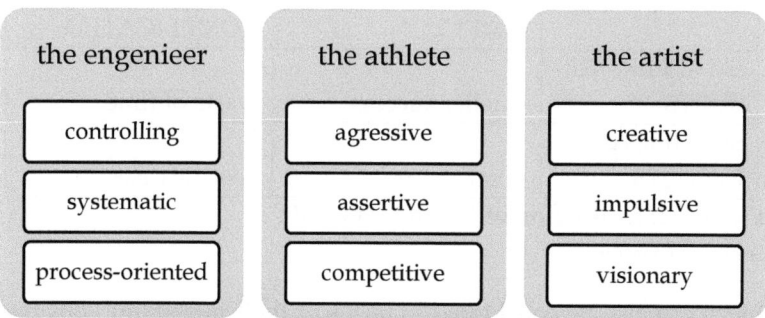

Figure 10: The "Imaginary Friends" technique
Source: own editing

When applying this method, we generate solutions and alternatives by calling on imaginary friends who can contribute to deeper reflection on the project with various aspects and perspectives.

Prototype: Selecting and developing a possible solution

Having considered the possible paths and solutions from many different perspectives and vantage points, in the next phase, the methods described above are used to select the most ideal, the best possible solution, which is then elaborated in detail and, finally, tested. (If needed, this phase is followed by fine-tuning, redesigning, reworking or moving on to other paths, since design thinking is iterative).

The first step is to think through the solutions and plans using the four-panel table presented in Figure 11. Based on this, we need to consider whether we expect smaller or larger results and how easy or difficult it is to implement the various ideas. Any idea that is expected to have smaller results and is difficult to implement can be rejected. The idea that is simple to implement and is expected to produce significant results is worth keeping and, in fact, should be chosen. Simple ideas which can lead to smaller results may be kept but not necessarily implemented, while complicated ideas which offer significant results should not be discarded but considered to be used later or in a certain situation.

	SIMPLE	COMPLICATED
SMALLER RESULTS	smaller success	waste of time
SIGNIFICANT RESULTS	great success	specific cases

Figure 11: Evaluation of the ideas raised
Source: own editing

Ideas can also be considered in terms of their interesting, positive and negative aspects (Figure 12). Thinking about these three features may also help in making a final decision.

the idea

Figure 12: Evaluation of ideas from three perspectives
Source: own editing

In the stage of selecting and creating a "prototype," examining it in terms of convergent and divergent parameters can be useful.

divergent
Effect: Will it produce an effect?
Interest: Are we interested?
Imagination: Is it a great idea? Is it powerful?
Urgency: Do we have to? What if we don't? Why not used so far?
Immediacy: Can we be quick enough to make it worth it?
Direction: Can it move us forward? Can it create new opportunities?

convergent
prize
time
feasibility
Plausibility: Can it be explained simply? Can our target audience understand it? Is it in line with our dominant values? Does it have any side effects? Is it supported by the leaders?
Usefullness: it is profitable? is it real need?

Figure 13: Evaluation of ideas based on convergent and divergent parameters

Source: own editing

In summary, we can inspect the chosen method, path, idea or solution with the help of the figure below.

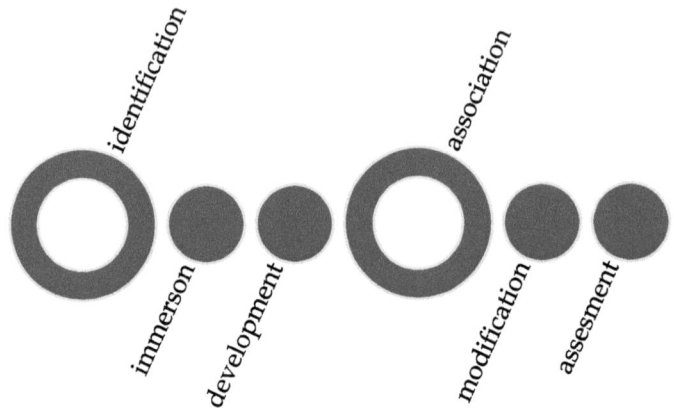

Figure 14. Overall assessment of projects
Source: own editing

References

Beck, U. (2003). *A kockázati társadalom – út egy másik modernitásba.* [The Risk Society – a Path to Another Modernity.] Budapest: Századvég.

Eberle, B. (1996): *SCAMPER: Games for Imagination Development.* Prufrock Press.

Folkman, S – Lazarus, R. (1988): Coping as a mediator of emotion. *Journal of Personality and Social Psycholgy,* 54:466-475.

Gulford, J. P. (1950): Creativity, *American Psychologist,* 5 (9):444-454.

Hankiss E. (1980): A magyar társadalom értékrendje. [The Values of Hungarian Society.] In *Érték és kultúra: összeállítás a TIT Szegedi IX. Művelődéselméleti Nyári Egyetemén elhangzott előadásokból,* (9):48-75.

Kopp M. (szerk.) (1980): *A magyar lelkiállapot.* [The Hungarian State of Mind.] Budapest: Semmelweis Kiadó.

Oláh A. (2021): *Érzelmek, megküzdés és optimális élmény.* [Emotions, Coping and Optimal Experience.] Budapest: Akadémiai Kiadó.

Reitter, P. – Wellmon, C. (2021): *Permanent Crisis. The Humanities in a Disenchanted Age.* Chicago: University of Chicago Press.

Rittel, H. W. J. – Webber, M. M. (1973). Dilemmas in General *Theory of Planning. Policy Sciences,* 4 (2):155-169.

Rowe, P. G. (1987): *Design Thinking.* Camridge: MIT Press.

Chapter 4
Higher Education and Social Responsibility

As discussed earlier, by the end of the 20th century, higher education institutions faced several new challenges. Most importantly, in response to changing socio-economic expectations, there emerged additional functions to their traditional activities, such as teaching and research. The "third mission" of higher education institutions, that is, the concept of social responsibility of higher education institutions or the "serving university" — as it shall be referred to synonymously in this chapter — fits in with these activities. In some views, the ideal type of university in the late 20th century is the so-called "third generation university," which implements the synergy of teaching, research and social responsibility. Others argue that in 21st-century higher education "fourth generation universities" have appeared as well, which not only respond to their socio-economic environment but also actively shape it.

This change of function and expansion has brought new challenges to the institutions. The third mission provides the links between higher education institutions and their environment, their activities and their impact on their social and economic environment (even by shaping it), and represents an institutionalised relationship with all partners in the non-academic world, having sustainability and the principles of environmental protection in view. Another third mission activity is the transfer of knowledge and experience accumulated in higher education that can promote the region's prosperity, increase its competitiveness and improve the inhabitants' quality of life. Furthermore, the third mission as an umbrella term includes all the patents, processes and products offered by higher education institutions: all the activities propagating science, and all the strategies, concepts and programmes they develop and help implement. Important elements of the concept include an active dialogue with society, the higher education institution's accountability to social and economic actors and having in sight the principles of sustainable human development are crucial elements of the concept of the third mission (Larrán—Andrades, 2013, cited in Jorge—Peña, 2017).

The chapter investigates the increasing functions of higher education institutions in the 21st century, with a specific focus on social responsibility/third mission activities. After studying various concepts, models and theories, two new models are introduced: one for the third mission activity of higher education institutions as a kind of core value ("3 M model"), and another one, the so-called 'fourth generation higher education model' that is representing a university which is not only reacting to social and economic problems but also actively forming them ("4 G model").

Higher education institutions and the third mission — theories and models

There are several milestones in the history of social responsibility in higher education (Dános, 2021). In the international regulatory context, it first appeared as the idea of a new social contract between universities and society in 1978, among the principles of the International Labour Organization. Accordingly, higher education institutions should provide education that takes into account societal needs, facilitates lifelong learning and plays a vital role in solving social problems to increase equality opportunities (Jorge—Peña, 2017; Site, 2019). This new function was named the third mission, which primarily responds to regional socio-economic needs. The Magna Charta Universitatum of 1988 is another significant milestone, highlighting European universities' values and emphasising their prominent social responsibility.

The concept of the Scholarship of Engagement, a forerunner of social responsibility in academia, was developed by Boyer in 1996. A few years later, the term university civic engagement emerged as a preliminary synonym for university social responsibility (Dános, 2021). In 1998, the World Declaration on Higher Education was published by UNESCO, highlighting the societal role of higher education as a whole. This was reinforced in 2009 by "The New Dynamics of Higher Education and Research For Societal

Change and Development," which, similarly to the previous document, emphasises the social responsibility of higher education.

The concepts emerging in the 2000s were dominated by the principles of sustainability and the image of the sustainable university. The growing involvement of higher education institutions was developed in the Helix models that were elaborated in these years: the Triple Helix, developed by Etzkowitz and Leydesdorff, as well as the Quadruple and Quintuple Helix models, further developed by Carayannis and Campbell (Etzkowitz−Leydesdorff, 2000; Carayannis−Campbell, 2012; Vass, 2012).

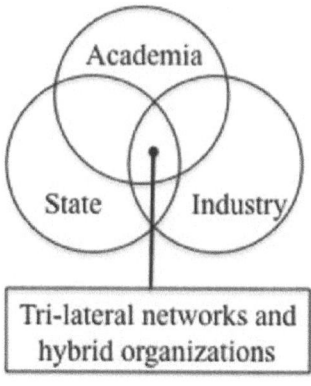

Figure 1: The Triple Helix model
Source: https://www.researchgate.net/figure/An-overview-of-the-Triple-Helix-Model-This-figure-demonstrates-the-dimensions-of-future_fig1_359398366

As illustrated by Figure 1, the model is based on the interconnection of three sectors, with an emphasis on interdependence (Etzkowitz−Leydesdorff, 2000). The intersection of the three includes hybrid institutions such as spin-off companies and incubators established in cooperation with higher education institutions. As a response to the late 20th- and early 21st-century phenomena, the three sectors not only fulfil their traditional functions but, by linking R&D&I activities, innovation, industry and academia, a complex model is implemented (Leydesdorff−Etzkowitz, 1998; Vass, 2012).

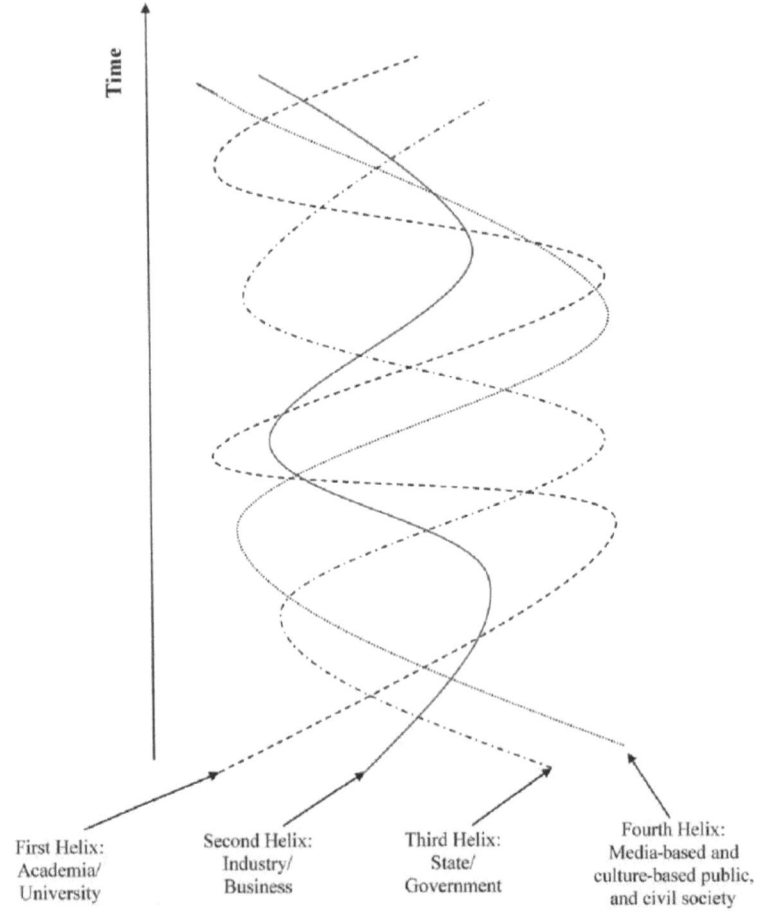

Figure 2: The Quadruple-Helix model

Source: https://www.researchgate.net/figure/The-Quadruple-Helix-Model-Source-Carayannis-and-Campbell-2012_fig4_318215853

With the Quadruple-Helix model, Carayannis and Campbell expand the Triple Helix model by including the social environment of the entire process, such as media- and culture-based public and civil society as well (Carayannis [et al.], 2012; Carayannis – Campbell, 2012, Vass, 2012). The model shows not only the social responsibility of higher education institutions but also their missionary, service-oriented activity much more emphatically.

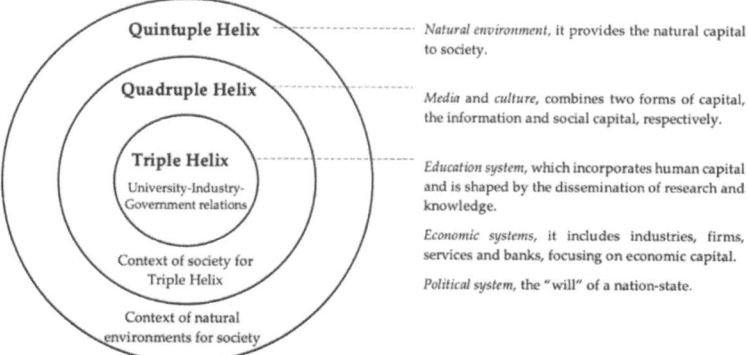

Figure 3: Quintuple Helix model
Source: https://www.mdpi.com/2071-1050/14/24/16499

In contrast, the Quintuple Helix model (Figure 3) also features the natural environment and thus includes the aspects of environmental sustainability as part of the third mission activity (e.g. environmental awareness and green technologies).

The third mission activity may also be regarded as a kind of public service development function (Gál, 2016). According to the renewed EU agenda for higher education adopted in 2017[3], the third mission activity of higher education encompasses all the diverse activities that institutions conduct for the social, economic, cultural, social and environmental development of their regional environment. In the past ten years, the significance of this role has increased to the point of being strategic (Sitku, 2019).

The previous sections have shown the ways in which expectations of higher education have changed and a new model of social responsibility, including a third missionary activity, is emerging. The following sections shall focus on how definitions of the third mission have changed, shaped and evolved. Jorge and Peña's study (2017) reviewed 15 years of theoretical literature to summarise concepts of social responsibility, formulating the following approach.

---

[3] https://eur-lex.europa.eu/legal-content/HU/TXT/PDF/?uri=CELEX:52017DC0247&from=SL.

Social responsibility is, on the one hand, "the capacity of the university to disseminate and implement a body of principles and general and specific values, by means of four key processes — management, teaching, research, and community engagement to respond to the needs of the university community, and in this framing, their 'country' as a whole" (Latin American University Builds Country Project, 2001, cited by Jorge—Peña, 2017:304). On the other hand, it is a guiding ethical guiding principle, "a policy of ethical quality of the performance of the university community (students, faculty and administrative employees) via the responsible management of the educational, cognitive, labor and environmental impacts produced by the University, in an interactive dialogue with society to promote a sustainable human development" (Reiser, 2008, cited in Jorge—Peña, 2017:304). Thirdly, "offer educational services and knowledge transfer based on the principles of ethics, good governance, respect for the environment, social engagement and the promotion of civic values (e.g. social justice, diversity, equity), on condition that they are accountable to society for their commitments to their stakeholders" (De la Cuesta, Porras, Saavedra—Sànchez, 2010, qtd. in Jorge—Peña, 2017:304). Fourthly, "the voluntary commitment of universities to include social, labour market, ethical and societal issues in their various core activities (teaching, research, governance, and environmental factors), which arise as external consequences of their operations and in respect of which they must also take into account the societal expectations of their stakeholders" (Larrán—Andrades, 2013, cited in Jorge—Peña, 2017:304). One vital element of all these approaches is attention to the aspects and principles of sustainable development.

According to Vallaeys (2014), in the third mission activity, the higher education institution is "open to dialogue, concerned about its local and global social and environmental impacts and active in promoting democratically produced science as a public and non-commodified good" (Vallaeys, 2014:96). Such a higher education institution "cares for its people and environment, aspires to worldwide academic diversity, rejects monopolies and the standardization of knowledge production, and encourages sustainable and equitable learning and research in communities of knowledge" (Vallaeys, 2014:96).

Reisinger and Dános (2015) emphasise that social responsibility must be present in all areas of the higher education institution. This would mean that sustainable development and social inclusion are also included in the curricula: in developing and shaping the environmentally and socially sensitive attitudes of students; in actions, scholarships and services promoting equal opportunities; in operating specialised colleges for advanced studies; in launching student support services (e.g. mentoring programmes); in teaching minority languages and cultural studies; and in the strengthening of educational links with civic organisations.

Higher education institutions and the third mission — Hungarian and international practices

Examining international practices between 2000 and 2015, Jorge and Peña (2017) found there was much to be done in education to facilitate a shift in attitudes towards third mission activities. The inclusion of social, ethical and environmental issues in the curriculum was poorly implemented by a considerable proportion of the higher education institutions studied, due to several factors, such as a lack of resources, appropriate approaches and sufficient knowledge of the issues (Sitku, 2019). In Jorge and Peña's view, improved knowledge of social responsibility can help the youth become more active citizens and more committed to public affairs.

In terms of research, third missionary activities can be linked to the mixed financing of higher education institutions and a decline in financial support from the state, since in this area, social responsibility primarily appears in the forms of greater cooperation with economic operators and emphasis on applied research. In addition, social responsibility is also present in the field of institutional governance: the accountability of higher education institutions, the establishment of good governance principles and the involvement of external stakeholders in governance processes can be viewed as the practical implementation of good governance and democratic principles. In line with these principles, it is essential to ensure a high number and wide range of stakeholders.

Regarding the fourth segment, the role of the community, social responsibility means promoting the emergence and dissemination of values such as diversity, equal opportunities, and social inclusion.

A significant international development to highlight is the University Social Responsibility Network (USRN), established in 2015, which currently incorporates 19 higher education institutions in the EU, committed to the consistent implementation of these goals. Hungarian practices have only been presented by a few studies so far (including Reisinger—Dános, 2015; Gál, 2016; Komlósi, 2015; Dános, 2021). Reisinger and Dános (2015) examined the social responsibility of three higher education institutions based on their strategic documents. Their research shows that social responsibility is increasingly present in the strategies of these institutions, albeit with different priorities. While at Széchenyi István University of Győr the emphasis is on cooperation with local and regional economic actors (perhaps due to the profile of the institution), the University of Miskolc focuses on compensating for disadvantages, and Kaposvár University on equal opportunities at large.

In his analysis of the third mission activities of the University of Pécs (2016), Gál discusses the important regional and urban, national and international projects that Pécs, as a committed serving university, has been involved in, in cooperation with other actors in the region. Komlósi's 2015 study examines the third missionary role of Széchenyi István University and highlights its commitment to the region. In his study of 21 higher education institutions, Dános (2021) claims that social responsibility was present at the level of both strategic documents and practice, though not to the same extent and intensity. The only critical observation is that in the majority of these institutions, the institutionalisation, communication and dissemination of third mission activities were deficient.

New concepts and models for the third mission and the fourth generation universities — the "3 M" and "4 G" models

In light of the above, the third mission of higher education institutions may be defined as follows (and thus be treated as a synonym of social responsibility): it encapsulates the links between higher education institutions and their environment, their activities and their impact on their social and economic environment (even by shaping it), and represents an institutionalised relationship with all partners in the non-academic world, with a view to sustainability and environmental protection, as well as good governance, diversity, social justice, responsible citizenship and equal opportunities, through the broadest possible involvement of stakeholders, bearing the principles of accountability and responsible management in mind.

This mission also cuts across the three main areas of higher education institutions' responsibilities: teaching, research and governance, and is manifested in a specific approach, in principles, practices and institutionalisation (e.g. equal opportunities office and disability coordinator). A committed, serving or fourth generation university is a higher education institution built on active interaction (affecting and actively shaping) with the social and economic environment it operates in, taking the principles and goals of the third mission broadly into account.

To illustrate these two definitions, two models have been created.

Figure 4: Modelling social responsibility/third mission activities as the core value of higher í institutions ("3 M model")

Source: Own editing

Figure 4 illustrates the theoretical and practical implementation of third mission activities. Within the first column, the *teaching function*, the activities listed above can be implemented with the help of six elements.

- Curriculum content: courses focusing predominantly on competency development; elective subjects with a focus on the principles of sustainability, equal opportunities, innovation, social justice, civic engagement and good governance.
- Teaching methods: new generation, problem-oriented teaching methods, based on the above principles, using cooperative, group and community work, and a project approach.
- Involvement of practitioners: involving social, economic and cultural actors in the teaching process, in line with the

profile of each course; dual training, short-cycle programmes, lectures for older people and bearing in mind the principles of lifelong learning.
- Approach: teachers and students committed to the activities listed above; sensitising training programmes with a focus on social responsibility and socio-environmental sustainability.
- Talent management and disadvantage compensation: differentiated instruction to accommodate student diversity, competency development modules, a system of colleges for advanced studies, mentoring and scholarships; training and courses to reduce early school leaving.
- practice-oriented education: an approach of applied learning; professional practice with peer organisations and partners.

In my view, the activities listed in the research function column do not require further explanation. The elements of the *management function*, on the other hand, do, especially because this column is rarely associated with the third mission of higher education institutions, even though it is another important area of its implementation.

- Accountability of higher education institutions: good governance and transparency.
- The principle of good governance: respecting democratic principles, with a view to the principles of civic engagement and accountability in leadership and governance, from macro to micro levels.
- Stakeholder involvement: the broadest possible involvement of social, economic and cultural actors in decision-making, to accommodate diversity.
- Approach: implementing the principles of sustainability, equal opportunities, innovation, social justice, civic engagement and good governance in leadership, management and decision-making.
- Institutionalisation: facilitating the practical implementation of third mission principles by establishing research and

service centres, departments and a system of desk officers and coordinators.
- Mixed financing: strengthening the presence of institutions on the market through good governance and applied research.

Figure 5 illustrates how all these are positioned in an economic and social environment.

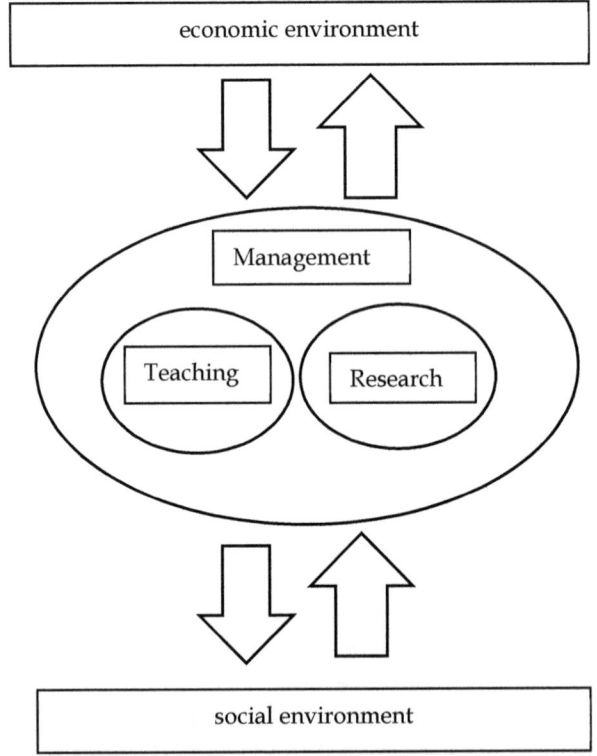

Figure 5: The committed, serving, fourth-generation university ("4 G model")

Source: own editing

References

Carayannis, E. G. – Barth T. D. – Cambell, D. F. J. (2012): The Quintuple Helix innovation model: global warming as a challenge and driver for innovation. *Journal of Innovation and Entrepreneurship*, 2, 1-12.

Carayannis, E. G.—Cambell, D. F. J. (2012): Mode 3 Knowledge Production in Quadruple Helix Innovation Systems. In. Carayannis, E. G.—Cambell, D. F. J.: *Twenty-first-Century Democracy*. *Innovation and Entrepreneurship for Development*. Springer Briefs in Business, 7:1–63.

Dános Zs. (2021). *A társadalmi felelősségvállalás formái a magyar felsőoktatásban*. [Forms of Social responsibility in Hungarian Higher Education.] Széchenyi István Egyetem. Doktori disszertáció.

Etzkowitz, H.—Leydesdorff, L. (2000). The dynamics of innovation: from National Systems and "Mode 2" to a Triple Helix of university-industry-government relations. *Research Policy*, 29 (2):109-123.

Gál Z. (2016): Egyetem és város. [University and City]. Educatio, (2):220–233.

Jorge, M. L.—Peña, F. J. A. (2017). Analysing the literature on university social responsibility: A review of selected higher education journals. *Higher Education Quarterly*, 71 (5): 302-319.

Komlósi I. L. (2015): A Cooperation Model for Higher Education and Industry: The Architecture of a Multi-Tier, Competence-Based and Practice-Oriented Education with Social Engagement. In: Fodorné Tóth K.—Németh B. (szerk.) (2015): *Tudás, társadalom, felelősség. Felsőoktatás és társadalmi felelősség: tudástranszfer partnerségi akciókban és elkötelezettségben.* Pécs: MELLearN- Felsőoktatási Hálózat az Életen át tartó tanulásért Egyesület.

Sitku K. (2019): *Egyetemi társadalmi felelősségvállalás*. [University Social Responsibility]. URL: https://www.researchgate.net/publication/331167085_Egyetemi_tarsadalmi_felelossegvallalas. (downloaded: 10/10/2024)

Reisinger A.—Dános Zs. (2015): *Egyetemi felelősségvállalás három magyar egyetem esetében*. [University Social Responsibility in the Case of three Universities]. https://tge.sze.hu/images/dokumentumok/K%C3%B6tetek%20%C3%B6sszes%20cikkel/2015.%20III.%20%C3%A9vfolyam%203.%20sz%C3%A1m_Cikkek/08_reisinger_adrienn_da nos_zsolt-2015-03.pdf (Downloaded: 10/12/2024)

Vallaeys, F. (2014): *University Social Responsibility: A Mature and Responsible Definition*. Higher Education in the World 5. URL: https://www.researchgate.net/publication/265501803_University_Social_Responsibility_a_mature_and_responsible_definition, https://doi.org/10.13140/2.1.2121.1523. (downloaded: 10/10/2024)

Vas Zs. (2012): Tudásalapú gazdaság és társadalom kiteljesedése: A Triple Helix továbbgondolása—a Quadruple és Quintuple Helix. [Fulfilling the Knowledge Economy and Society: Thinking Beyond the Triple Helix—the Quadruple and Quintuple Helix]. In: Rechnitzer J. -Rácz Sz. (szerk.): *Dialógus a regionális tudományról*. Széchenyi István Egyetem Regionális- és Gazdaságtudományi Doktori Iskola; Magyar Regionális Tudományi Társaság, Győr, pp.198-206.

Chapter 5
The Role of Community Coaching in Social Innovation Projects

In the previous chapters, we have seen how applied social science and sociological approaches can be utilised in generating and managing social innovations, how divergent thinking and dealing with "wicked" problems can be combined with an innovative approach, and how higher education institutions in the 21st century can contribute to the common good and the development of a more liveable society through their third missionary role (which in many cases is realised through facilitating social innovations).

In this chapter, I outline how "community coaching" — a rather under-discussed aspect in theoretical literature today — may contribute to the successful implementation of social innovation projects.

Coaching and community coaching

Coaching is a personal, interactive and highly focused developmental relationship. It facilitates individuals' and/or organisations' effective achievement of goals and overall efficiency. It is a goal- and results-oriented development that helps better understand internal and external resources and connect them more creatively. Coaches are professionals who assist and support coachees in reaching their goals successfully.

Coaching has several trends and models and its theoretical literature is extensive. The present chapter does not aim to list or discuss all these but to place community coaching among the various types of coaching. The coaching process can be classified according to various aspects: (1) the trends and approaches; (2) the subject of coaching, the number of coachees and the nature of the challenge. In terms of the latter, we can differentiate between self-coaching, individual coaching, group and organisational coaching and — as it shall be discussed later in the chapter — community coaching.

Community coaching is a development process in which a systemic change takes place in a community context, through and with the empowerment and participation of community members (Emery et al, 2011). It is a form of assistance and support that helps communities reach their goals by exploring individual and community resources and taking into account individual ambitions. The phrase 'individual ambition' is used here because I firmly believe that the role of a community coach is to find those people within the community who, with adequate support, can act as 'ambassadors' of the community and later as facilitators, who actively contribute to achieving their common goals.

Community coaching can also be defined as a process of mobilising and effectively organising (i.e. transforming into objectives and tools) resources and skills that are already locally available at the level of the individual and the community. The community coach does not provide answers but uses capacity building and change management to facilitate the community in finding their own adequate responses to the challenges.

Community coaching builds on mutual and common learning. In this respect, it can be linked to the notion of the learning organisation: an organisation's or community's continuous, resilient, proactive adaptation to changing circumstances and new challenges. It builds on synergies in the service of both individual and community goals and development, goals and development.

The community coach can see the bigger, fuller picture; present collaboration as a value; align opportunities, goals and priorities; and determine the possible paths for development.

The diagram below illustrates the place of community coaching among the various coaching processes.

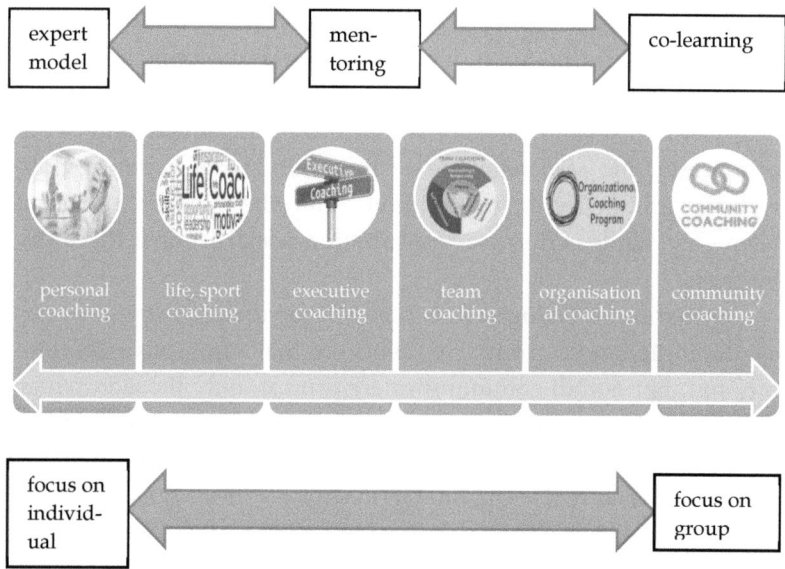

Figure 1: Different types of coaching
Source: Emery et al, 2011. Own editing.

Community development and community coaching

This section aims to highlight the similarities and differences between community development and community coaching, especially because—as we shall see—the distinction between the two is unclear. First, let us take a closer look at community development and some of its key concepts.

The concept of community has been defined in many ways (Varga—Vercseg, 1998). These definitions highlight its wide range of qualities, such as being local and organised around a common set of values, involving a sense of a shared destiny and developing a certain community identity. According to American sociologist Talcott Parsons, the notion of community can refer to shared actions of individuals as well as their similar location (in online space, however, locality is no longer an essential element, as it is possible to create and actively participate in communities virtually). In Ferdinand Tönnies's *Community and Civil Society*, (1887), the community is also a symbol of coziness and neighbourliness, a notion that the author contrasts with the concept of society. He views the latter as some artificial formation in which individuals exist much more independently of each other than in the former.

German sociologist Max Weber makes a distinction between community and association: in a community, social action is motivated by an intellectual or traditional attitude based on a sense of belonging, while in the case of association, social action is driven by interests.

American sociologist Robert K. Merton distinguishes between a community and a group. He points out that a group is a community but that not all communities are groups, only those in which members interact with each other. Although people belonging to a community are held together by common social standards, in many cases there is no real social interaction among them; thus, they cannot be regarded as a group. In contrast, philosopher Ágnes Heller believes that communities are superior to groups, since, as opposed to group membership, being a member of a community is a choice made by individuals on their own account.

In *Közösségfejlesztés* [Community Development] (1998), Ilona Vercseg and Tamás Varga emphasise that community is a concept that carries value and an organisation that serves the well-being of both its members and society through the collective and freely determined actions of its members. Communities are essential for the functioning of democracy, since it is through and by them that citizens can shape and form democracy effectively.

In addition to all the above, community action fills a gap and is capable of exercising a kind of control vis-à-vis governments in power. Its gap-filling role primarily means that it can respond flexibly to emerging social needs and societal challenges, and that in many cases, community members contribute to the common good with voluntary work.

Community development at the local and community level also means that with the strengthening of local communities, a civil framework of social publicity is established to control governments in power. Viable communities can cooperate in creating and shaping the rules of local society by setting up local formal and informal organisations.

The methodology of community development is not written in stone—it is highly flexible. It depends on the ingenuity, skills and experience of the community developer to decide which method to use. The first phase of community development always starts with reaching out to and involving the local population, followed by determining the needs, gaps and possible directions for development. Throughout the development process, more and more individuals and enterprises eager to make a contribution are involved, then potential partners are convinced and join in to solve problems through the development of knowledge and skills.

The development process can be divided into the following phases (Varga—Vercseg, 1998):

- Phase 1. Creating "motion": This means bringing together local community actors (civilians, communities, shapers of local public life) and kindling their interest in local development, motivating them to become active participants in local community life.
- Phase 2. Exploring the situation: This phase involves mapping human resources, as well as the economy and education at the local level. This is essentially an economic and social stocktaking exercise, which also aims to explore what may be expected in the future, given the current situation.
- Phase 3. Exploring the opinion, capacity and motivation of the community: In order to map development opportunities with the involvement of the locals, a detailed survey of the population needs to be conducted.
- Phase 4. Planning: This entails deciding which actions are to carried out in the short, medium and long term.
- Phase 5. Community building, launching community projects: Cooperation in the local community means developing, creating and shaping a community. Therefore, community development already starts in the phase of project planning.
- Phase 6. Finding and engaging internal and external partners: The project and visions for the development of the area need to be presented to the local and county government, other communities, and potential partner institutions

and organisations. The tasks should be divided among community members and it should be discussed who will be responsible for what and how, who will be in contact with whom and how.
- Phase 7. Coordinating and managing: Since by this stage the project becomes highly diverse and complex, it requires an organisation, a group or a person to coordinate and manage it.

The methods used in community development are as follows:

- Activating methods (e.g. self-organising circles, dialogue circles, knowledge pools)
- Methods to generate local publicity (generating news, documenting events, sharing them on various communication platforms)
- Methods to improve cooperation (promoting intersectoral cooperation)
- Economic development methods (setting up for-profit and nonprofit organisations, cooperatives and associations)
- Methods to explore and get to know the localities (SWOT analysis, problem tree and objective tree, questionnaires, interviews, field research, etc.)

Distinguishing community development from community coaching is not easy but perhaps not necessary either, because the two can act synergistically with and inspire each other. As pointed out above, community development is primarily an activity whereby a community can get assistance and support to organise itself through its own resources and competencies. The goal of both community coaching and community development is to help achieve a kind of empowerment, a process at the end of which the coach or community developer withdraws from the processes, that is, makes the community 'self-propelled.' Community coaching puts great emphasis on finding local ambassadors who, supported by personal coaching, are efficiently equipped to act as catalysts for the community.

Community development aims to organise internal resources more effectively, with the community coach helping to formulate new goals and match resources (existing and external) to them. The latter also supports the community in exploring alternative paths and solutions by shaping thinking and has a transformative effect, i.e. it can lead to new values, paths and a higher level of community integration.

A community coach should have the following skills:

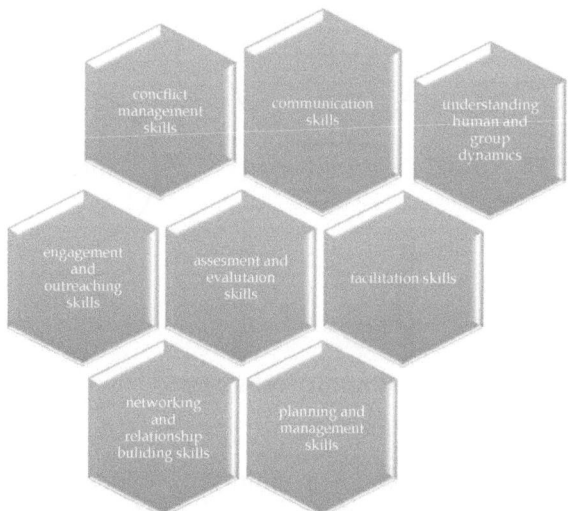

Figure 2: Skills required for community coaching.
Source: Emery et al, 2011. Own editing.

A community coach's primary objective is to help the community see its goals more clearly. This is achieved by asking good questions. In comparison, community development, as mentioned above, focuses on exploring and organising a community's competencies and knowledge. Community coaches also introduce tools that can help the community develop a more realistic view of the situation and can facilitate decision-making, levelling up and handling difficulties. Therefore, community coaching places great emphasis on change management and capacity building.

The community coach also plays a role as a bridge, as illustrated by Figure 3.

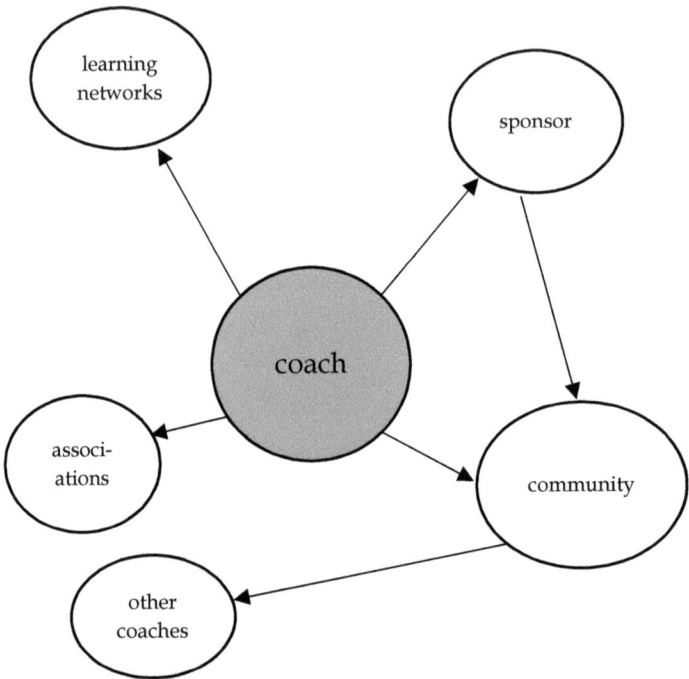

Figure 3: The coach-community ecosystem
Source: Emery et al, 2011. Own editing.

The coach becomes part of a multi-stakeholder ecosystem and serves as a link between other coaches and the community, other organisations and the community, and other members of the network and the community.

In addition to all these outlined above, community coaching has six other characteristic features (Emery et al, 2011).

The first feature is readiness, a kind of 'ready-to-launch' state, the state of openness to everything. This allows for being open to the resources and competences of the community and to be able to assess their status and condition.

The second characteristic is the world of relationships. It involves the building of trust and confidence in the community, as well as identifying the important actors in the life of the community and how they are connected, what their functions are. It also means exploring the resources of each actor and planning how to build on them so that the community could benefit from them. In the case of relationships, it is important to map what members think about cooperation, with whom and on what issues they usually work. It is also crucial to build strong and weak connections between the community and other sectors and actors.

Third: reflection or self-reflection. It entails reflecting on whether the planned intervention is workable, what is truly useful and what is not. Continuous feedback is vital in order to correct any possible mistakes in time.

The fourth essential aspect is achieving the right results. Short- and long-term results can maintain the motivation of the community members. Everyone should know the goals and the paths leading to them, and how progress will be measured. For real results, realistic plans are needed. It is important that the coach can help the community and its members move from passive bystanders to active doers.

Resilience is the fifth element: building resilience in the community, promoting the ability to adapt to change, a kind of 'learning organisation mindset.' It also means that core values need to be made clear and adhered to in order to ensure that the foundations of community identity can be maintained amid change.

The sixth, final attribute is reach. The term represents the implementation of plans, achieving the goals, generating change and overcoming resistance.

The diagram below shows the six phases of community coaching.

1. Early start-up phase:
Goal: Finding a shared vision
How do we see the community then and now (e.g. 2-5-10 years from now?)
How can we do something like never before, while staying on track?
How can we bring the strength and energy within us to the surface?

2. Early start-up or gear-up phase
Goal: A valid description of the current situation
Exploratory methods:
What strategies shape the current situation?
What strengths do we have that work well in some places?
What can we learn from the past X years?
What stands in the way of a better future?
What uncertainty factors are there?
What opportunities for the future are there?

3. Gear-up phase
Goal: Understanding the mindset and attitudes that limit change
What can we do to make plans a reality?
How can we move towards change?
How can we get people to work together rather than compete?
How can we take the view of the organisation's goals?
Developing strategies and solutions
Actions
Long-term goals and small steps with an impact
Roles in implementation

4. Action and learning phase
Goal: Implementing new programs and plans
Where are we? What have we achieved? What do we need to refine?
How is management working?
How involved are people?
How is all this communicated?
Are there any unexpected factors?
How are we dealing with external actors?

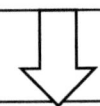

5. Acceleration and momentum-building phase
Goal: Optimising effectiveness and impact
Sustainability of results achieved so far, actors and tasks

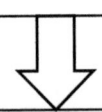

6. Sustaining phase
How will all this be sustainable in the long term?

Figure 4: Phases of community coaching

Source: Emery et al, 2011. Own editing.

As illustrated by the above figure, the phases of community coaching are quite similar to organizational development processes. Change management and capacity building are essential elements in community coaching, just as in organisational development. The community coaching process is dominated not by circularity but by linearity; that is, once a goal is set, the next step is to move towards this goal with the help of resource management to optimise effectiveness and impact. As opposed to community development, the community coach is an active player in these processes, not someone who sits on the sidelines and facilitates processes that can more or less unfold on their own as well.

Using community coaching to implement social innovation projects

As we have seen earlier in this book, although there is no common definition of social innovation, there are indeed similarities between the different approaches. Accordingly, social innovation

- is an initiative generally generated at the micro level, bottom-up, with community participation;
- aims to meet a social need,
- often a need that cannot be met by the market;
- emphasises cooperation in generating these in various groups in society and thus a higher level of cooperation can be achieved;
- aims to solve problems and needs that arise in society;
- leads to the emergence of new attitudes, values, social relations and possibly new structures as well in the process;
- results in increased community well-being and an improved quality of life;
- and its outcome may take several forms: know-how, product, concept, service, technology, organisation or novel interconnections.

All this shows what a local community can do or achieve through community coaching. It can

- work in innovative ways;
- create a common product (product, service, etc.);
- link with other organisations and partners, creating weak and strong connections, bridges, etc. between itself and other entities;
- disseminate innovative solutions and thinking patterns in the community;
- develop innovative solutions to address emerging social problems;
- get to the next level, that is, become better, more efficient, more integrated;
- transform from informal to formal at the organisational level;
- establish a social cooperative or other formal frameworks of self-organisation;
- improve the quality of its members' lives;
- become self-sustaining in certain areas;
- and transfer the results of the process, in whatever form, as good practice.

References

Emery, M.—Hubbell, K.—Polka, B. M. (2021): *A Field Guide to Community Coaching*. South Dakota State University. https://openprairie.sdstate.edu/sociology_grad_guide/8/

Tönnies, F. (1887): Community and Civil Society. Publisher: German History Intersections.

Varga A. T.—Vercseg I. (1998): *Közösségfejlesztés*. [Community development.] Parola Kiadó Közösségfejlesztők Egyesülete és a Magyar Művelődési Intézet

Chapter 6
Case Studies

The second part of the book introduces the reader to the practice of social innovation through five case studies, all of which present projects that built heavily on the social responsibility of higher education institutions, that is, all of them were implemented in a higher education setting. Thus, these case studies describe the implementation of projects that may be models for linking the two areas. Each of the five case studies offers an insight into a different field.

6.1. Predicting and Managing Local Conflicts in the Framework of a Social Innovation Project

The project entitled "Rug or patchwork? Social forms and norms of coexistence, peaceful and conflictual coexistence in multicultural contexts," implemented between 2017 and 2020, made a long-cherished dream come true. Our idea was to build and implement a social innovation project to analyse and predict social conflicts, and to find possible solutions to various conflicts. We planned to (1) examine social conflicts at micro, meso and macro levels as well, and create a municipal-level database based on existing data at the regional level; then (2) narrow the research focus to 50 municipalities to be able to provide even more details and (3) conduct in-depth qualitative research in five selected municipalities for a better understanding of the conflicts, thereby continuously adding quantitative and qualitative data to our database. The project also provided opportunities for the spatial modelling of conflicts and displaying them on digital geospatial maps, thus indicating the reasons for their development and their characteristics.

In addition to its methods and collaborations, the innovativeness of the project lay in aiding decision-makers (mayors, local communities, groups) by providing a "formula" of the typical processes of social conflicts, and demonstrate how to solve, resolve and use them for development. The social innovation model for conflict prediction and management resulting from our targeted applied research may also be used effectively in the future to develop a sustainable, data-based model supporting economic, social, business and public policy planning and decision-making, which could be applied in other lagging regions of the world as well.

The case study presented below discusses the background to this social innovation, the research concept behind it and the major activities of the three-year project.

The basic concept of the project

The basic research aimed to better understand and systematically describe the nature of social conflicts in the Northern Hungary region: how they are addressed and what possible solutions could be offered to social conflicts of different types and natures. Our primary objective was to provide a constant, reliable, multidimensional, empirical data-based tool (methodology, procedure) that could support public policy decisions and thus help stop the negative escalation in regions that are extremely underdeveloped and unable to recover on their own — all within the framework of social innovation, with the involvement of national and international partners. The methodological repertoire (know-how) developed can simultaneously collect and manage social, economic and socio-psychological information, thereby facilitating the assessment of potentials for conflict, the modelling of conflicts, as well as timely intervention and conflict management in socio-economically lagging regions.

Over the project's lifetime, this development was carried out in the North-Hungary region along with the transfer of experience, thus implementing it as a good practice.

Predicting and managing conflict is a vital condition for economic recovery and job creation, not only with regard to market mechanisms but also for state, regional and local public works, public employment and community-based economic programmes. Successful conflict management based on predicting local conflict is thus an indispensable component of local cooperation, the sale of local products and other similar social and economic innovations in particular.

Conflicts, social conflicts and conflict research — the theoretical background of the project

Although conflict research is a current topic internationally, no research is available on the sociological prediction of social conflicts. There is only one study using psychological methods to measure conflict, especially ethnic conflict (Bordás – Huncik, 1999).

The structural and socio-cultural context of conflict has been studied by several sociologists (Dahrendorf, 1994, 1997; Lenski, 1984). Figure 1 below summarises how various social theories deal with social conflict, presenting the latter from two aspects. On the one hand, it highlights both those that occur in everyday life and those regarded as more serious, such as inter-group and class conflicts. On the other hand, as indicated, conflict can be interpreted as something that occurs infrequently, or is frequently and widespread.

Structuralist-functionalist social theories belong to the so-called theories of harmony. K. Davis and W. E. Moore, two of the most prominent proponents of this theory and authors of the study that developed and defined it, argue that everything in society is functionally necessary. The system of social inequalities has evolved and is needed because it fundamentally reflects social utility and significance and, in turn, motivates individuals to attain a higher social status. The theory does not take conflicts into account much, regarding them as exceptional cases.

Marxist conflict theories view conflict as indispensable for the development of society. Class struggle is the driving force behind social change and development, and without it, a just society cannot be achieved.

In Figure 1, the theories belonging to group III are connected by the fact that they analyse conflicts at the level of everyday life and focus on how they can disrupt, from time to time, the order of society and community, and what necessary function these actions may have.

Finally, Group IV includes ideas that have in common a better understanding of the causes, nature and drivers of conflicts and similarly derive them from the causes.

highly signifi-cant	I. Structural functionalist	II. Marxist (critical sociology)
everyday	III. Micro-functionalist, applied sociological (the institutionalisation of conflict theory)	IV. Approaches focusing on conflict functions Neo-Weberian sociology (critical sociology) (the institutionalisation of conflict theory)

Figure 1: Theories of society and conflict
Source: Csizmadia, 2014.

As indicated by the summary analysis above, some theories assert that conflict is necessary for achieving a chance at a better life. Life chances are influenced by a combination of factors. Conditions for individual action, that is, the options for action that can be chosen in a certain situation (as Dahrendorf calls them) are structurally determined (Dahrendorf, 1994). Motivations and goals for individual action, which arise from the lifeworld's patterns of worldview and life (Dahrendorf calls these ligatures and distinguishes between obligations and rewards) are socio-culturally determined. Oftentimes, an individual or a group of individuals can only improve their life chances at the expense of others. Thus, having no possibility of achieving better life chances at the individual level leads to the emergence of inter-group conflicts and resolving conflict with violence usually result (Bordás—Huncik, 1999; Allport, 1977; Hunyady, 1996; Tajfel, 1981.)

Conflict commonly manifests itself as conflict between majority and minority (Csepeli 2006; Csepeli-Örkény-Székelyi 1997). Any society, including local societies, can be divided into majorities and minorities based on any socially relevant aspect and any aspect that affects the position of individuals and their groups in a system of social inequalities may be considered socially relevant. One's position in the system of social inequalities is closely related to the range of life chances, and the size of space for individual actions, which, as explained earlier, is what makes conflicts necessary. Realistically, this structural situation leads to potential conflict between the majority and minority. It is also quite prevalent that the majority fails to recognise the reasons for the deterioration of its own situation or the lack of the improvement expected and, instead of exploring the interconnections, it resorts to a scapegoating mechanism (Csepeli, 2006, Tajfel, 1981; Hunyady, 1996; Horowitz, 1985).

Conflict may also be analysed as related to social change and social innovation. Two basic types of social change can be distinguished: disruption and innovation. Disruption is usually achieved through resolving conflict with violence, such as wars, revolutions and acts of terrorism. Social innovation, on the other hand, means the internal transformation of existing relations, where conflict management is carried out in a controlled way: individuals with similar interests and aspirations organise themselves and start social movements. Social movements thus generate and help implement social innovation.

Some of the cases that emerge or can be predicted as conflicts are neither adequate nor inadequate conflicts—they are pseudo-conflicts (Buda, 1974). When pseudo-conflicts are predictable, the task is to help recognize non-zero outcomes, to prove that there are social situations in which expanding the space for individual action and achieving a more favourable position in the allocation of goods—that is, achieving a higher status in the system of social inequalities—can be achieved not solely at the expense of others but by cooperation, and thus everyone involved in the pseudo-conflict can commonly benefit from the achievements.

Another central theme of conflict research is to investigate at what level conflicts and disagreements appear (Csizmadia, 2014). They can emerge at the level of the individual (as a kind of internal conflict or between individuals), the group (within and between groups) and the community (within and between communities); as well as between organisations, social strata or municipalities; regionally, nationally or globally. Our research aimed to explore potential conflicts and disagreements at each of these levels, but with a primary focus on certain settlements.

Another possible aspect of conflict research is the area or field where conflict emerges, which may be listed as follows:

- demographic (e.g. the ageing of a settlement or generational conflict)
- religious
- ethnic
- private (family, friends)
- related to the labour market, health or education
- territorial, related to residence or neighbourhood
- political, related to representation
- economic, business-related

Conflicts may manifest as hostility, malicious rumours or gossip, avoidance, discrimination, physical aggression, persecution, exclusion and genocide.

They may be characterised by dichotomies such as overt vs. covert, violent vs. non-violent, community-wide vs. affecting only a few, resolved vs. unresolved and functional vs. dysfunctional.

The aims and activities of the project

As a result of economic and social changes, social conflicts have increased and deepened in the region of Northern Hungary. Several misconceptions about conflicts have been perpetuated. Many see every conflict as a source of danger, a negative phenomenon. Others incite conflicts even when they have no basis, to improve life chances. Conflicts often arise between parties that have no real conflict of interest but can in fact work together to assert their interests effectively. As shown in the previous section, conflicts can emerge between different structural groups; between rich and poor, or they can be ethnic, national, generational, gender or economic conflict, or other types that this very research intended to focus on.

Our project applied an interdisciplinary approach to exploring ongoing, covert and potential conflicts in the Northern Hungarian region's settlements. Based on the research results, a conflict prediction system and a digitalised database were developed, which laid the foundation for the development of a supportive, conflict management human services network.

The method and system of predicting social conflicts we developed and put into practice in the course of our project are unique in the world for a number of reasons. Our project was based on the assumption that conflict prediction is not a marginal objective, nor is it simply an issue for those directly affected by conflict. Predicting and adequately managing conflict at the level of society as a whole is a fundamental concern politically, economically, and population-wise, determining the quality of life. Therefore, we developed a social informatics system in the Northern Hungary region that is capable of predicting social conflicts early on and providing public policymakers with an appropriate conflict management and decision support tool. The system can also function as a map of needs and public security, and thus be important and useful for businesses wishing to invest in the region, that is, it can also be used for business purposes. Our project can help prevent conflict from turning into mass violence, transgressing the institutional framework of regulated conflict management, as well as unnecessary, avoidable conflicts dominating society. We focused on forms of conflict management that both help avoid violence and stimulate social innovations that create a favourable environment for economic development and make actors in the conflict realise that the best way to achieve better life chances is through economic activity, successful entrepreneurship and successful employment. Predicting and managing conflicts is an important prerequisite for economic recovery and job creation, not only in terms of market mechanisms but also regarding state, regional and local public works, public employment and community-based economic programmes. Our project facilitates keeping conflicts manageable and preventing them from becoming a factor for large-scale migration.

Another innovative element of the project is that during its implementation, we trained and operated a crisis intervention team, which made it possible to intervene in social conflicts and manage them to foster social development. With the help of the team, we could determine the appropriate method for conflict management in time, implement a controlled form of conflict management and, by resolving the conflict with consensus, the social innovation generated could be achieved with the participation of the stakeholders, which led to improved life chances. As a result, social cohesion and integration were strengthened, and positive social and economic changes were initiated in the region.

The implementation phase included a continuous mapping of countries with similar problems as potential partners for expanding the social conflict prediction system to Europe.

The research phase, that is, the mapping of local conflicts, was carried out using a complex array of quantitative and qualitative methods. This ensured obtaining reliable data at macro-, meso- and micro-levels and creating a detailed picture of social conflicts, as well as identifying typical forms of conflict and thus being able to provide and implement the know-how of dealing with them, with the involvement of stakeholders.

The objectives of the project outlined above were achieved through the following chronologically listed activities:

- A workshop for preparing the project, setting up the team
- R&D&I training for the professional team (research management, communication of research results, networking)
- Starting the development of a database on conflict areas:
    o obtaining a T-Star database, desk research of the data
    o obtaining other available databases (municipal, county, regional), desk research of the data
    o producing a social informatics map based on the data
- First wave of large-scale quantitative questionnaire research to understand the nature of social conflict:
    o selecting 50 municipalities in the region
    o having a sample of 1000 people
    o design and testing the questionnaire
    o preparing the SPSS data files
    o recruiting interviewers
    o training interviewers
    o consulting the questionnaire

- coding the questionnaires
- data entry into SPSS
- data cleaning
- preparing the tables
- analysis
- First wave of expanding the database:
  - expanding the database, entering the data of the first wave of the survey
  - developing the social informatics map
- Identification, analysis and management of social conflicts through ethnomethodological report in 5 selected municipalities by contacting opinion leaders:
  - research to gain a deeper understanding of the nature of typical social conflicts through qualitative fieldwork and social intervention in the 5 municipalities selected
  - visits to the municipalities every two weeks, continuous contact in between visits
- Continuous processing of reports, the second wave of expanding the database
- Starting work on curriculum development for a 30-hour "Social conflicts and their management" course
- Hosting guest lecturers from abroad on the theme of the project
- Travel to the University of Tallinn to study research work on social conflict management
- Organising a domestic conference to present the project results
- Publication
- Second wave of large-scale quantitative questionnaire research:
  - the questionnaire survey with a population sample of 1000, repeated at the beginning of the second year of the project
- Data from the second wave of the questionnaire survey used for the third wave of expanding the database
- Identification, analysis and management of social conflicts through ethnomethodological report in 5 selected municipalities by contacting opinion leaders:

- research to gain a deeper understanding of the nature of typical social conflicts through qualitative fieldwork and social intervention in the 5 municipalities selected
    - visits to the municipalities every two weeks, continuous contact in between visits
- Continuous processing of the reports, the fourth wave of expanding the database
- Completion of curriculum development work on the project theme (30 hours of training)
- Organisation and publication of research materials
- Hosting guest lecturers
- Organising an international conference to present the project results
- Publication
- Travel to the University of Barcelona for the dissemination of the project
- Participation in an international conference
- Setting up and training a crisis intervention team:
    - Preparation for crisis intervention and mediation activities in the 5 municipalities selected with the involvement of opinion leaders to ensure that social conflicts are socially useful and generate a positive turn
- Crisis intervention in the 5 municipalities selected
- Identification, analysis and management of social conflicts through ethnomethodological report in 5 selected municipalities by contacting opinion leaders:
    - research to gain a deeper understanding of the nature of typical social conflicts through qualitative fieldwork and social intervention in the 5 municipalities selected
    - visits to the municipalities every two weeks, continuous contact in-between visits
- Organisation and publication of research materials
- Finalisation of a social informatics map of the social conflicts identified
- Hosting guest lecturers
- Publication

The relevance of the project and the research towards EU development agendas

It is common knowledge that the development of convergence regions requires economic and social renewal. One of the obstacles to economic renewal today, and increasingly in the future, is the widening and deepening of social conflicts. Although conflicts may become a driving force for development, their inadequate management, particularly the prevalence of violent solutions, endangers social cohesion and peace. Maintaining social cohesion and ensuring social inclusion and integration are indispensable for the functioning of the economy, the ability of municipalities to retain their population and the improvement of the quality of life of people living in convergence regions.

Our project aimed to utilise the theoretical and methodological knowledge accumulated at the university, the skills acquired in identifying various social problems and competencies in conflict management by identifying and predicting social conflicts in the region and developing training programmes and services for effective conflict management. During its implementation, the team's research activities effectively prepared young researchers and university students qualified as research candidates for both further research activities and the practical implementation of the supportive human services developed by the project. The conflict prediction system and database developed during the project make it possible to provide conflict management human services in an entrepreneurial framework, and enable the multiplication of R&D&I activities and their wide dissemination to other regions struggling with similar problems.

The indirect impacts of the project include the utilisation and expansion of the university's knowledge base (through human resources and service development), contributing to the creation of a knowledge-based economy and strengthening cooperation with the business sector. In the course of the project, existing knowledge and competencies were utilised and reproduced in an extended form. New teaching materials were developed, new national and international contacts were established, scientific events were organised and publications were launched. The quality of human resources improved and strengthened, particularly the skills and competencies of young researchers and university students. All these benefited the declared practical orientation of our training courses and improved the labour market position of young graduates.

As the wider impact of the project, conflict situations in the region of Northern Hungary (as well as those with a similar profile) can be managed within a controlled framework and perceived conflicts arising from misinterpretation of the situation can be avoided. The institutionalisation, regulation and adequate management of social conflicts strengthen social cohesion, which has a positive affect on the settlements' ability to retain their population, the inhabitants' quality of life and economic recovery.

Economic recovery is a result of investors considering security as a crucial aspect of their investments, as they are more willing to invest in places with potentially no social conflict or 'explosions.' Social conditions also influence the state of the workforce and economic performance. The former can perform better if it is not preoccupied with conflicts. In addition, solvent demand is higher in areas where social conflicts do not threaten the good progress of life. Finally, predicting and managing conflict builds trust, and strengthens collaboration and cooperation skills.

References

Allport, G. W. (1977): *Az előítélet*. [The Nature of Prejudice.] Budapest: Gondolat Kiadó.

Buda B. (1974): *A közvetlen emberi kommunikáció szabályszerűségei*. [The Rules of Direct Human Communication.] Budapest: Animula Kiadó.

Bordás S.–Huncik P. (1999): *Feszültség előrejelző Rendszer*. [Tension Prediction System.] Dunaszerdahely: Nap Kiadó–Pozsony, Márai Sándor Alapítvány.

Csepeli Gy. (2006): *Szociálpszichológia*. [Social Psychology.] Budapest: Gondolat Kiadó.

Csepeli Gy.—Örkény A.—Székelyi M. (1997): Szertelen módszerek. In: *Szöveggyűjtemény a kisebbségi ügyek rendőrségi kezelésének tanulmányozásához*. [Unconventional Methods. In: A Textbook for the Study of the Police's Handling of Minority Cases.] Budapest: COLPI.

Csizmadia Z. (2014): *A Társadalmi konfliktusok kutatásának elméleti megalapozása – új nézőpontok és kutatási irányok*. [Theoretical Foundations of Research on Social Conflict—New Perspectives and Research Directions.] Magyar Tudomány, 11.

Dahrendorf, R. (1994): *A modern társadalmi konfliktus*. [The Modern Social Conflict: An Essay on the Politics of Liberty.] Gondolat Kiadó: Budapest.

Dahrendorf, R. (1997): Társadalmi stuktúra, osztályérdekek és társadalmi konfliktus. [Social Structure, Group Interests, and Conflict Groups.] In Angelusz R. (szerk): *A társadalmi rétegződés komponensei. Válogatott tanulmányok*. Budapest: Új Mandátum Könyvkiadó.

Davis, K—Moore, W. E. (1997): A rétegződés néhány alapelve. [Some Principles of Stratification.] In Angelusz R. (szerk): *A társadalmi rétegződés komponensei. Válogatott tanulmányok*. Budapest: Új Mandátum Könyvkiadó.

Horowitz, D. L. (1985): *Ethnic groups in Conflicts*. Berkeley: University of California Press.

Hunyady Gy. (1996): *Sztereotípiák a változó közgondolkodásban*. [Stereotypes in Changing Public Thinking] Budapest: Akadémiai Kiadó.

Lenski, G. E. (1984): *Power and Privilege: A Theory of Social Stratification*. UNC Press Books.

Tajfel, H. (1981): *Human Groups and Social Categories. Studies in Social Psychology*. Cambridge: Cambridge University Press.

6.2. "Creative Region" — Using Innovation to Reduce Regional Disadvantages

One of the best examples of the third missionary role of higher education institutions — discussed in detail in Chapter 4 — is our project implemented in the framework of the Institutional Excellence Program for the Higher Education, presented as a case study in this chapter.

As mentioned earlier in the book, generating, facilitating and implementing social innovation requires expertise that is, in many cases, present in the surroundings of the project, often in the form of a higher education institution. The project described here, implemented in three phases from 2018 to December 2025, may be regarded as a real social innovation. Why? When preparing the application at the end of 2017, we thought that if a city can be 'smart,' then a region can be 'creative.' The idea was to implement the programme in a disadvantaged, convergence region, the development of which is of key importance in a series of actions taken to address regional, social and economic disparities. We firmly believe that a lack of resources, be it human or economic, can often be compensated for, at least partially, by creativity. This is why we named our series of projects Creative Region.

Its innovative character can be found in a number of project elements. First, it aims to combine locally available resources, knowledge and skills to improve quality of life, which is a characteristic feature of innovative projects. Second, by exploring geographical and cultural resources, the project also helps regional economic development and contributes to the development of tourism as well. Third, it capitalises on the role of providing outreach and service, one that a higher education institution, especially in a disadvantaged region, must inevitably take on. Fourth, it helps disadvantaged settlements to 'put themselves on the map,' that is, to improve their national and international visibility (this is achieved by creating an app and Wikipedia articles on the settlements involved, written in English, Slovakian and Hungarian and based on scientific research). Fifth, it strengthens relations among the state, local authorities, civil society organisations, churches and the higher education institutions involved.

The aim of the project

The project started in 2018 and was implemented in three phases, i.e. in three application periods.

The first phase took place from 2018 to 2019. Relying on the research experience of social and cultural innovations in the region, Creative Region I explored the areas of new social and cultural innovations and their potential for implementation by building an interdisciplinary team of experts from the fields of economics, social sciences, health, law and humanities, involving PhD students and young researchers, and utilising national and international partnerships.

The model concept developed focused on sustainability and regional development. The core region was a micro-region of 25 municipalities, known as "Dark Abaúj." The aim was to map economic, cultural and human resources in a complex, innovative new structure, as a result of which we created a mobile application called "Abaúji Mutató" (Abaúj Index). The app is suitable for the dissemination and widespread implementation of the project results, as well as for finding potential investors and business partners, and for connecting the settlements involved to facilitate building a network. Furthermore, it can function as a tool for tourism development by indicating museums and cultural heritage sites and recommending hiking trails. Another significant product of this phase is a local innovation indicator, which shall be discussed in the next case study.

The second phase, Creative Region II, was implemented between 2019 and 2021. Based on the results of Creative Region I, the model and know-how previously produced to map cultural assets for socio-economic innovation was further developed, disseminated, verified and field-tested with the help of our interdisciplinary team of economic, social, health, legal and humanities experts, formed in the previous phase of collaboration. We aimed to continue mapping the economic and cultural resources located in the target area, in a complex new structure, by identifying the relations, focal points and possible centres of the area under study, including the municipality of Encs as well. Further developing the Abaúj App, and maintaining and updating the data were also priority tasks. In addition, to increase the visibility of the settlements even more, with the help of historians and other social researchers we created Wikipedia articles describing 26 municipalities in Hungarian and English, and, in the case of border settlements, in Slovakian.

The third phase covers the period between 2022 and 2025. Building on our previous achievements, in its first year the CR III project continued feeding back, developing and disseminating the results of the pilot programmes in Abaúj County through various scientific, community, school and cultural events. From the second year on, we have adapted the research to the Edelény District and internationalised the results. The adaptation involved a complex questionnaire survey of the population of 25 municipalities in the Edelény District and interviews with formal and informal decision-makers, institution and company management, the heads of civil society organisations and church leaders — the same methodological repertoire as the one applied in the first phase. The research results were channelled into a new application, Borsod App. One of the priorities was to contribute to improving the research conditions, involving PhD students and young researchers throughout the entire duration of the project. The direct and indirect economic development solutions (business start-ups, local product branding, creative tourism, education equalising programmes, cultural asset repository, mobile app) emerging from the research activity will create the conditions for networking and cooperation among the actors through the transformative power of social innovation. Publication activities will aim at the widest possible dissemination of the results (in the settlements and to the general public alike) and professional publication. As another novel element, the project places great emphasis on the local adaptation of creative tourism and developing the concept of smart tourism adapted to the area.

In many ways, the project fits into the third mission of higher education. First, it involves the university's engagement in regional cooperation and its contribution to improving the quality of life of the people living in the region. Second, it also organises social innovation actions, inclusion programmes and regional awareness-raising events. Third, it facilitates tourism development by increasing the visibility of the municipalities in the project area. Fourth, it searches for cultural assets in the regions concerned and makes them available to the local population, thereby aiding the consolidation of local identity. Fifth, it contributes to increasing R&D&I activity, another vital element of the social missionary role of higher education.

Activities and results of the three phases of the project

Creative Region I (2018-2019)

The model concept developed focused on sustainability and regional development. In our approach, the model has two levels: it examines the research questions identified in the county and the core region as well. Based on previous research and corresponding to the existing Kosice-Miskolc route and the Kosice-Miskolc motorway route under construction, we defined "Dark Abaúj," a microregion of Abaúj as the core region. Our goal was to map the economic and cultural resources at the examined levels in a complex new structure.

During situation analysis and modelling, the following tasks were determined and implemented:

- Developing the concept of a cultural assets repository (delineating the content elements, creating a 'script,' database design, GIS solutions and template documentation on a georeferenced digital map of the cultural assets identified).
- Conducting empirical studies with quantitative and qualitative tools of social science research, in the form of a questionnaire survey of the population in the 25 municipalities concerned and interviews with local formal and informal leaders. Based on these and by analysing statistical data,

creating a regional data warehouse to explore the resources, competencies and knowledge present in the municipality.
- Producing thematic geographical economic maps of the region.
- Creating an SPSS database to store research data and be used for further analysis.
- Producing image films and 10-15 page descriptions for each of the 25 municipalities.
- Assessing hidden cultural assets.
- Analysing the social innovations implemented in the region and their impact.
- Conducting a health survey of the school-age and adult population — both representing a potential workforce — and launching screening programmes for prevention.
- Mapping the current state of public education institutions that will shape the next generation, and the possibilities of a much-needed shift in pedagogical culture to compensate for disadvantages.
- Developing and testing the index "Local Innovation Potential" to measure the innovative capacity of municipalities.
- Assessing the online visibility of all the municipalities involved, with the help of the SentiOne programme.
- Compiling a collection of famous people originally from the region.
- Carrying out a political analysis of the region (election results, political activity, etc.).
- Conducting a historical mapping of the region.
- Exploring and producing 30-40 detailed descriptions of the built heritage.
- Producing 15 image films and more than 150 photos of the settlements, organised in a photo library.
- Creating a downloadable application called Abaúj Index to present the statistical and demographic data, and cultural and geographical values of the 25 municipalities.
- Disseminating the project results at several national and international conferences and in several publications.

Creative Region II. (2019-2020)

Building on the results of Creative Region I, we further developed and tested our innovation model, continued action-oriented social interventions and work on increasing the visibility of disadvantaged settlements.

The objectives were achieved through the following activities:

- Continuing the development of a social innovation model, know-how, which was not only finalised but also spread and disseminated during the period of the undertaking. Assistance in training potential stakeholders to implement similar social innovations (through innovation mentoring, complex innovation workshops, and an international conference). Development/updating/expansion of Wikipedia entries for 25 municipalities in the area studied. The Hungarian-language glossaries were standardised and extended for the 25 municipalities surveyed, English-language glossaries were edited and a Slovak-language glossary was created for the border settlements, in accordance with the editorial principles of Wikipedia. The natural and geographic material was expanded based on the previous project and the new research. Data on the history of the settlements, their political image, economic actors, famous people, cultural values and socio-demographic data were added. This activity was considered important since, although the municipalities do have Hungarian-language entries of some sort, their quality and content are questionable, despite the fact that their presence on the site can guarantee visibility both nationally and internationally.
- Maintenance, expansion and dissemination of the Abaúj App, created in the previous programme:
Exploring the use of the app for economic recovery, increasing its impact in stimulating the economy and tourism, and ensuring its wide publicity.
- Increasing the socio-economic innovation potential of the area through activities, complex workshops, international conferences and professional events that help strengthen

local identity and businesses; identify potential entrepreneurs; promote entrepreneurship; reinforce a sense of community, interdependence and solidarity; and improve the quality of life.
- Training and advice on innovation skills and generating innovation as vital elements of the programme in three areas. (1) Information training, demonstrating the importance of and opportunities for regional development, and possible ways of becoming an innovator. Our aim was to familiarise municipal leaders with innovative thinking and the practical implementation of the theory of "mayor = innovator." (2) Mentoring a business and supporting measures for economic development. After a full analysis of the situation (people to be involved, locations, business ideas), the programme aimed to examine start-up challenges for one enterprise, transfer relevant knowledge and prepare a business plan and/or a feasibility study. (3) Compiling and making available methodological material on the start-up and management of an enterprise, and supporting its implementation with consultancy.
- Smart Village Pilot Programme:
  In two settlements in the district examined, our goal was to create the feasibility of smart solutions and a complex approach thereto to help make the everyday life of the entire community more convenient and efficient (e.g. business promotion, municipal management, surveillance and security, free internet access, dealing with official matters and sharing information).
- Implementing a mentoring programme, using gamification:
  In some groups of young people in the district studied, we applied life coaching and used gamification to help them identify their resources and competencies, set goals and address problems. We believe that gamification is a useful tool that supports the development of values in a playful way.

- Preparing information materials on social innovation opportunities for the mayors of the municipalities involved and elaborating the legal framework thereof.
- Implementing monitored health screening programmes involving the adult population.
- Developing lifestyle, recreation and health promotion programmes, and expanding the variety of related training programmes offered by the university.

CR III (2022 - 2025): cultural and social innovation, sustainability and creative tourism

In the framework of the Creative Region III project, we first implemented the activities detailed below in Abaúj County, and then extended our model to another disadvantaged district, Edelény. In addition, we developed a new application, Borsod App, to disseminate our latest results in a clear and accessible way to the general public.

In the period between 1 January and 31 December 2022, these commitments were implemented through the activities detailed below.

In the second phase, between 1 January 2022 and 31 December 2023, the pilot programmes were further developed and extended, and the results were fed back and disseminated through various scientific, community, school and cultural events in the Abaúj district.

- 5 public dissemination forums organised to strengthen local identity in the micro-region.
- Continuing the organisation of travelling exhibitions in schools (7 venues).
- Organising a cultural-musical-literary event at Fáy Castle.
- Implementing an education equalising programme to eliminate social disadvantage and providing related consultancy.
- Mentoring businesses and providing support for writing business plans.
- Supporting the implementation of the Smart Village programme (with a focus on e-administration).

- Population health assessment, health protection and screening programmes, with women and young people (girls aged 10-14) as the main target group.
- 5 campaigns and media events to promote the social impact of the research results so far.
- Methodological training to increase publication activity.
- 1 scientific workshop organised and 66 publications produced.
- In the upcoming, third phase from 1 January 2023 to 31 December 2025, we will adapt the developed model concept to the Edelény District through the following activities:
- Conducting extensive sociological, demographic, historical, family history, cultural, economic, intergenerational, innovation and health science research in the Edelényi District.
- Developing and establishing a regional data warehouse for the municipalities, including interactive georeferenced digital maps.
- SPSS database based on the survey results of the settlements.
- Conducting research on cultural heritage and museology in the area, and mapping the related civil and church organisations.
- Testing our basic model for measuring social innovation potential in the new municipalities involved.
- Examining the links between social sustainability and social innovation.
- Producing image films and a photo library for 25 municipalities in the Edelény district.
- Extending the County Repository of Values with the research results.
- Developing the Borsod App.
- Disseminating the results to the population and organisations of the county as part of the university's third mission.
- Follow-up of the methodological renewal of public education institutions.
- Interactive sessions in public education institutions in the region.

- Workshops and lectures on local history in the municipalities to present the results so far, to strengthen local identity and for community development.
- Innovator training and education.
- Organising an international summer university in the summer of 2025.
- Contributing to local fairs, festivals and events linked to the region.
- Survey on competencies as a service provided in the region, on a pilot basis.
- Organising two Experience Days and Sports Days for 8th-grade and high school students at the University of Miskolc.
- Preventive health promotion programme developed by the Faculty of Health Science, based on monitored data to improve the local population's health.
- Small-scale tourism development based on local resources and professional knowledge.
- 1 final conference, 1 workshop per year (3 in total), 66 publications per year.

The above lists of activities demonstrate that our ongoing project is highly complex and includes several innovative elements, which have been presented earlier. An important aspect of the project is that in addition to conducting research, it also implements the results in practice to help reduce the marginalisation of a disadvantaged region and improve the quality of life of the people living there.

6.3. Local Innovation Potential—The Basic Model and Its Testing

The present case study presents the methodology developed during the previously discussed Creative Region project, which is suitable for measuring the local innovation potential, that is, the innovation capacity of a settlement.

As mentioned in Chapter 1, when working on the Local Innovation Potential (LIP) Index I present in this study, I drew upon existing theories and models of social innovation. The complexity of the LIP index developed in the Creative Region project derives from building on qualitative and quantitative data and research methods. Therefore, it is simultaneously based on social scientific methods traditionally considered "soft" and "hard." As a starting point, I focused on the fact that settlements and communities can be multifaceted, which means that the LIP index shall also be such. The LIP index is befitting for taking local specificities into account and, by doing so, presenting a precise description of the current situation and characteristics of a settlement, together with its future potential and directions in development.

In the following, I first introduce the principles and guidelines along which the LIP model was developed (in the context of pre-existing models). Second, I examine the applicability of the model to five settlements in Abaúj (Büttös, Fáj, Fulókércs, Szemere and Hernádpetri), all disadvantaged and located in Northern Hungary.

Local Innovation Potential Index—the basic model

The basic model was formed in the context of previously existing models. It was important to design it with several pillars (as, in an ideal case, settlements also have more than one strength to draw upon) and to reflect one of the most important characteristics of innovation: diversity. The model had to be suitable for applying quantitative and qualitative methods and approaches, and for building on various data sources. It was likewise vital that the indicators of the model could be available and measurable in every settlement studied. Therefore, we observed the criteria of validity and reliability, as well as the need for a standardized measurement tool.

The model presented below rests on four pillars: (1) local courage (LC); (2) human resources potential (HR); (3) economic potential (EP) and (4) cultural and natural "resources" (CNR).

The first pillar appears in the model because we wish to emphasise that social innovations tend to come from a grassroots perspective and usually offer a novel solution to existing social problems or challenges. Compared to the innovation measurement tools introduced above, local courage is a new component, as other research did not identify such processes.

The second pillar, HR is a well-established component of measuring innovation potential. Although different in operationalisation, human resources are usually part of any measurement of innovation capacity. The same can be said about the third component, economic potential.

As for CNR, we applied the approaches of the Collection of Hungarian Values[4] and its focus on the cultural and natural resources of the settlements. These resources strengthen local identity and help form bonds.[5] This is also a common component of models measuring local innovation capacity and is usually considered a common environmental factor. However, the CNR component presented here is more than that. We believe that in order to balance disadvantages we shall draw upon the cultural resources and strengthen local identity.

Within each pillar, the dimensions and the possible indicators to be measured are indicated. When forming the model, we built on the concept that correlations revealed by quantitative data and their hidden meaning can further be examined by qualitative approaches. Thus, one part of our data comes from statistics and documents (decrees, strategies, reports), another part from surveys, and the rest from qualitative interviews and field notes. The source

---

[4] www.hungarikum.hu
[5] www.hungaricum.hu

of our data and its qualitative or quantitative nature are shown in the figure below.

Each dimension or component is measurable by seven (7) indicators. The maximum value of a dimension/component is 35. All seven indicators are measured on a five-point scale. To standardise the index, we transformed the dimensions (with their maximum value of 35) to a 100-point scale (where 35 means 100 per cent).[6] The value of the components of the LIP has been calculated accordingly.

The maximum value of LIP is 140 (4 pillars, 7 indicators, each measured on a five-point scale). The maximum value of 140 was also transferred to a 100-point scale to achieve a standardized LIP index.

1. Local courage (LC)
<ul><li>co-operation (qualitative, interview)</li><li>good practices in education (qualitative, interview)</li><li>grant activity (quantitative, received EU grants/person 2012-2018)</li><li>novel solutions – economic (qualitative, interview)</li><li>participation in community events (quantitative, survey–percentage)</li><li>participation in the work of civil society organisations (quantitative, survey–percentage)</li><li>number of non-profit organizations (quantitative, TeIR[7]–percentage)</li></ul>
2. Human Resources Potential (HR)
<ul><li>proportion of higher education graduates (quantitative, TeIR-number of higher education graduates/100 persons)</li><li>percentage of "active individuals" (quantitative, TeIR – percentage of 18-54 years old)</li><li>abortion (quantitative, TeIR – percentage of abortions in relation to birth between 2011 and 2013)</li><li>infant mortality (quantitative, TeIR – percentage in relation to the average of 2001-2013)</li></ul>

---

[6] The index was standardised with help from Attila Z. Papp.
[7] TeIR: Országos Területfejlesztési és Informatikai Rendszer (National Regional Development and Spatial Planning Information System, https://www.teir.hu

	• ageing (quantitative, the proportion of elderly [over the age of 65] to other age groups) • local knowledge (quantitative, survey – percentage) • vehicles (quantitative, TeIR – number of passenger cars/ 100 persons)
3. Economic potential (EP)	
	• number of entrepreneurship (/100 persons; economic sector, types) (quantitative, TeIR – 100 citizens) • Net income per person (quantitative, survey – per person) • infrastructure (quantitative, TeIR) • unemployment rate (quantitative, TeIR – percentage of unemployed in the age group of economically active citizens) • local tax (quantitative, TeIR – local tax income /100 persons) • employment rate (quantitative, TeIR – proportion of employed people to citizens in active age) • migration (quantitative, TeIR – migration balance)
4. Cultural and natural resources (CNR)	
	• natural values (qualitative, interviews, observations) • values of the built environment (qualitative, interviews, observations) • intellectual property (qualitative, interviews, observations) • artefacts (qualitative, interviews, observations) • local artists, groups (number of groups and individuals, type of the groups) • famous people (qualitative, interviews, observations) • local traditions (quantitative, survey – percentage)

Figure 1: The basic model of Local Innovation Potential (LIP)
Source: author

About the settlements

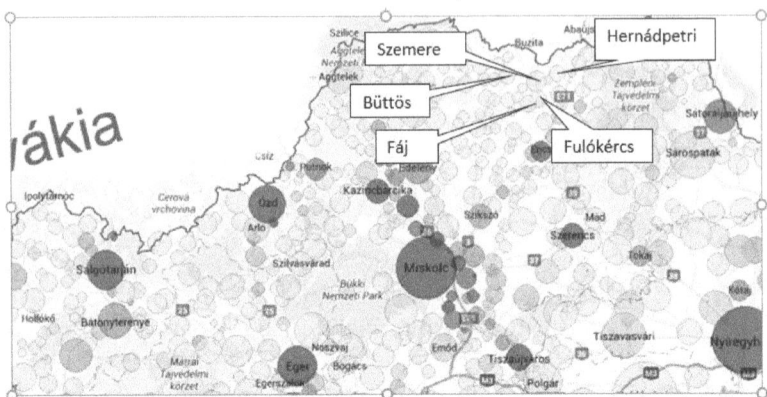

Figure 2: The research locations

Büttös is a one-end village, situated in the valley of the Rakaca stream, in the district of Encs. It has a population of 189 (as of 2018). It is an ageing settlement (ageing index in 2016: 390,9). It is under the jurisdiction of the notarial district of Krasznokvajda. Medical assistance is provided by the GP practice in Krasznokvajda. The settlement does not have a kindergarten or school. Children attend kindergarten and school in Krasznokvajda, taking the bus provided by the village. The village is surrounded by apple orchards; yet the apple cannot be processed in the village but has to be transported to hundreds of kilometres away after harvesting to be processed. No grocery stores, cafes or bars can be found here. In the past five years, 8-10 houses were purchased by Slovakian citizens. The settlement does not have a church, only a bell tower which is part of the former school building. At present, 32 people work as public workers in Büttös. Farm products produced by the public workers are sold in the village, thus providing some income to the local government.

Fáj is situated in the district of Encs, 50 km from Miskolc. It has all the characteristics that Ladányi and Szelényi (and others) list as typical of ageing communities with a high proportion of Roma inhabitants, located on the outskirts, which is also true for another settlement studied, Hernádpetri. In terms of socio-demographical data, Fulókércs is similar as well, but this particular settlement is special in some regards, as described later in the study.

These settlements started to decline in the 1970s, resulting in an incomplete society without local intellectuals. As a consequence, a lonely, declassed local society developed, characterised by depression, hopelessness and no future.

Fáj has a population of 457 (as of 2018). In the national census of 2011, 3% of the inhabitants identified as Roma but the estimated numbers are much higher. In the past, the settlement belonged to the Fáy family. Their memory is gone, only the classical mansion built in 1750 remains. Since the 1990s, the building has been managed by The National Trust of Monuments for Hungary. It has a joint local government with Szalaszend. The village has a Roman Catholic church.

Fulókércs has a population of 415 (as of 2018). The village is mostly inhabited by Roma people; thus, it is not characterised by the ageing of the population. Out of the 113 households in the village, 60 % (71 households) have running water and only 29 houses are connected to the gas supply system. In the framework of the current housing program, 6 social rentals are being built.

The village has a kindergarten with 51 children and an elementary school, offering education from the first to the fourth grade.

Two inhabitants are college graduates, 10 people graduated from grammar schools and 30 finished vocational training. Some of the youngsters attend secondary school in Encs, Tokaj Debrecen and Szikszó. Since 2012, a special afternoon school for children with special needs has operated at the settlement.

The centre of the village is the "House for the Elderly," as locals tend to call it, equipped with a soup kitchen and a library. The community centre is full of life and events. The village has a Calvinist church and a nice football field with dressing rooms. In terms of local transportation, the village has little to offer. The village bus runs hundreds of kilometres every day. In addition to two grocery stores, the village also has a nicely renovated GP's office but no GP to set up practice. A childminder is available regularly. Currently, 100 people work in the public work program breeding livestock, producing crops and renovating buildings. The 2-3 acres of cultivated land provides the villagers with almost everything. The inhabitants are hard-working people. Several civil society organizations tried to help over the years, some of them with success. The mayor is Roma and has a very good reputation in the village.

Hernádpetri is a small one-end village in the northeast part of the Cserehát region, near the Slovakian border. In 2018 its population was 259. In terms of public transportation, the village is hard to access; there is only one bus between Hernádpetri and Encs available for travellers. The village is inhabited mainly by Roma people, that is, only a few non-Roma households can be found there. The number of run-down hoses is striking. Several households do not have access to running water. Electricity is supplied on a prepaid basis. Its late baroque-style Roman Catholic church, built in the 18th century, is in a dangerous condition.

Basic grocery items are hard to purchase as the only grocery store in the village has rather hectic opening hours. Medical assistance is available once a week and serious illnesses or emergencies are treated in Encs. With no kindergarten or elementary school in the village, the children attend primary school in the nearby Hernádvécse. Most of the inhabitants are undereducated, job opportunities are scarce.

Szemere is situated 5 km north of the Slovakian border, in the district of Encs. Encs is 18, and Miskolc is 60 kilometres away. Since 2013 the settlement has had a joint local government with Szalaszend. The nearest train station is 13 km away, in Méra, with access to main roads. The only form of public transportation is the bus with a few services daily. More than half of the inhabitants are Hungarian (58%), 42 % are Roma. In 2018, the village had a population of 417. A little more than half of the population belongs to the age group of 18-54. The proportion of elderly people (above 60) is 11,67%. Outward migration is common and only a few new settlers move to the village. The low number of local intellectuals is a serious problem.

The number of registered businesses in the village is 5, but only one local person is employed. In 2011 and 2012, 76 people worked in the public work program. The local government is the largest employer, as businesses cannot provide job opportunities for the locals. In the framework of the public work program, a pig farm, providing meat for the local soup kitchen, was established, greenhouses were built, state-owned agricultural fields were received and wood furnaces were purchased. As part of the public work program, a small number of people produce pasta and bakery goods, also for the local soup kitchen and the children in school. A fruit procession unit was also set up to process apples and make apple juice and in 2015 a Social Cooperative with six employees was founded for these purposes. The local government provides help for the elderly and food for those in need. Since February 2001, a village caretaker service has been offered.[8] The inhabitants rely on the service and use it regularly. The village caretaker currently uses a Volkswagen minivan to transport villagers. Although the settlement does have a doctor's office, the post is vacant. Medical services are provided in Szalaszend, so people seeking medical help need to travel on their own or use the village caretaker's transportation service. There are two grocery stores in the village (one is part of the grocery store chain 'Coop', the other is in private ownership) and one bar (more like a café). There is a post office as well. There used to be a community centre in the village, too, but its building is now used by the school and its absence is palpable. In terms of educational institutions, the settlement has an elementary school and a kindergarten as well.

Adaptability of the model in the settlements examined

The pattern of the local courage index for the five settlements in Abaúj is illustrated in the following figure.

---

[8] The village caretaker service is a social service provided for the inhabitants of disadvantaged settlements. It offers transportation services and administrative help, among others.

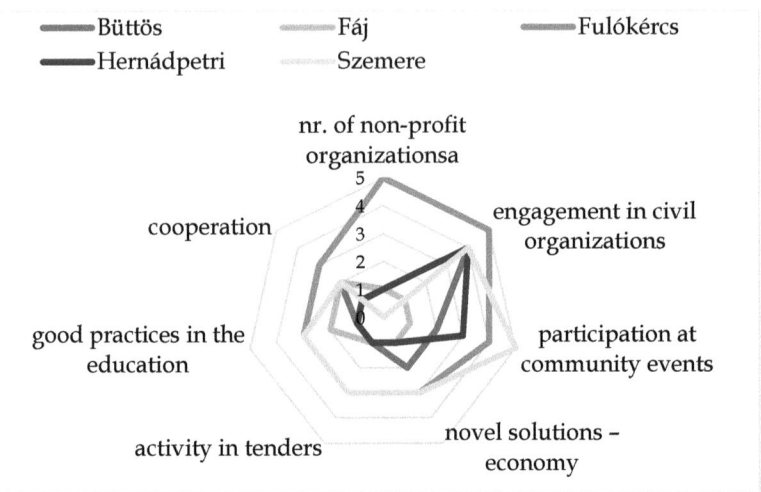

Figure 3: The "pattern" of local courage (LC)
Source: the author

As shown in the figure above, the most significant element of local community activity is engagement in civil organizations. It is the most defining factor in the measurement of activity among the inhabitants. This element is especially strong in Fulókércs. As we have already pointed out in the description of the settlement, Fulókércs has a strong, solid community with the current mayor as its driving force. Participation in local community events is a similar item and is especially prominent in Szemere. While Szemere is different from Fulókércs in many respects, they are similar in terms of their mayors being the centre of local community life. It is an interesting characteristic of Szemere that the local intellectual elite are not local per se, that is, the cultural life of the village is organized by the head of the kindergarten who lives in Miskolc, while the schoolmaster lives in Szemere. There is a small group of decision-shaping intellectuals in Szemere, whereas Fulókércs has an active Roma community, instead with strong community ties, suitable to form a base for presenting and delivering patterns.

The figure above also indicates that in terms of LC, two settlements have significant roles, and these are neighbouring villages. One is populated exclusively by Roma people, while the other only has a few Roma inhabitants.

The community of Büttös, described as an ageing and poor village, is active in civic society organizations. It must be noted, though, that due to its ageing population, the number of non-profit organizations is low. We can conclude that the social activity of the locals does not have organizational frameworks, they rather engage in spontaneous actions. The same is true in Szemere: although there are no civil society organizations, the population still lives an active community life.

In many ways, Hernádpetri is a contradictory settlement. Community activity in the village is not high; it has a rather poor image of communities characterised as cultures of poverty. Meanwhile, owing to civil society organizations coming from outside, there are occasional integrative, community development programs aiming to compensate for disadvantages.

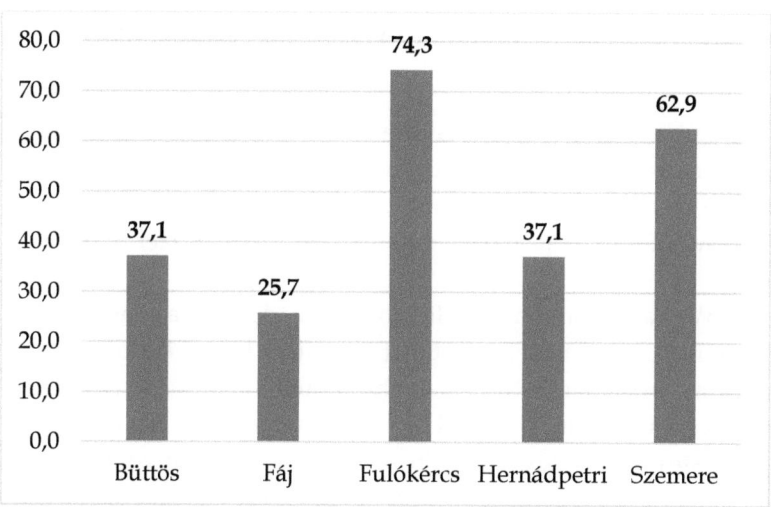

Figure 4: The values of local courage index (LC)
Source: the author

Figure 4 shows the CC index at the five settlements. The figure confirms our findings: Fulókércs ranks the highest in local courage, followed by Szemere. Fáj has the lowest index: out of the 7 indicators 5 received only 1 point.

The next "component" of local innovation potential is human resources potential (HR).

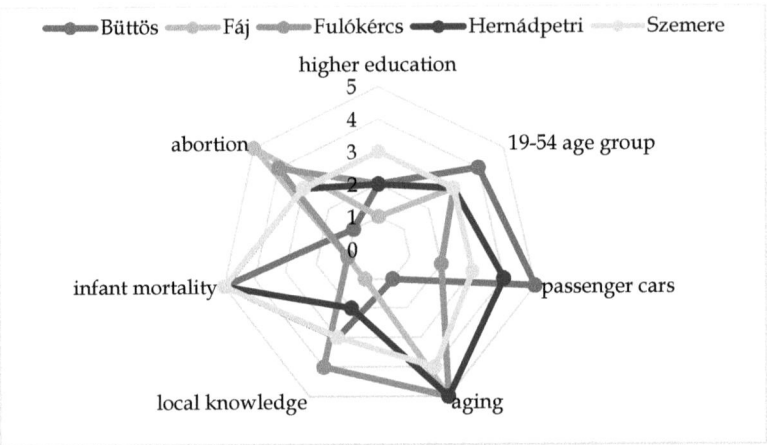

Figure 5: The "pattern" of human resources potential (HR)
Source: the author

The figure clearly reveals that the human resources potential does not vary as much as the local courage index, for which Szemere and Fulókércs achieved higher results. Szemere also shows good results in terms of human resources potential, and so does Hernádpetri as well.

We have mentioned earlier that Hernádpetri is a contradictory settlement. It is due to the fact that the village has a high proportion of Roma inhabitants: the village has a more favourable age structure (ageing rate in 2015: 31,11/5), the number of higher education graduates is very low (1,7% in 2016), it has a negative migration potential, and the settlement does not have any educational institutions. The proportion of the 19-54 age group is relatively high, just like the number of passenger cars, which may also be regarded as a sign of vitality (and indicates that due to the lack of proper public transportation, the locals need to have cars). The village has a very favourable ageing rate: the number of elderly is low compared to the number of children. The infant mortality rate is also favourable in Hernádpetri. As pointed out earlier, several development projects have been initiated at the village by outsiders and the fieldwork detected some resistance toward new projects among the locals.

Szemere also shows good results in terms of this indicator. Among the villages in focus, Szemere has the highest proportion of higher education graduates, and the ageing and infant mortality rates are also good.

Fulókércs achieved good results in terms of local courage and, as we can see, the local knowledge is significant as well. It means that the locals have skills and knowledge in many areas and forms, such as sewing, embroidery, folk art, crafts, wood-carving and metal-working.

Figure 6 shows the value of the HR component at each settlement. Hernádpetri and Szemere have the highest value of human resources, followed by Fulókércs and Büttös. Fáj falls behind the others.

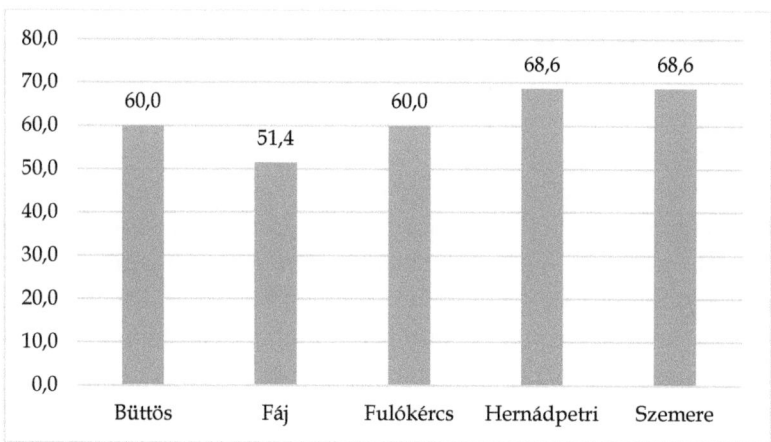

Figure 6: The values of human resources (HR)
Source: the author

The third pillar of local innovation potential is economic potential (EP).

As indicated by Figure 7, Fáj and Hernádpetri have lower, while Fulókércs, Büttös and Szemere have higher economic potential.

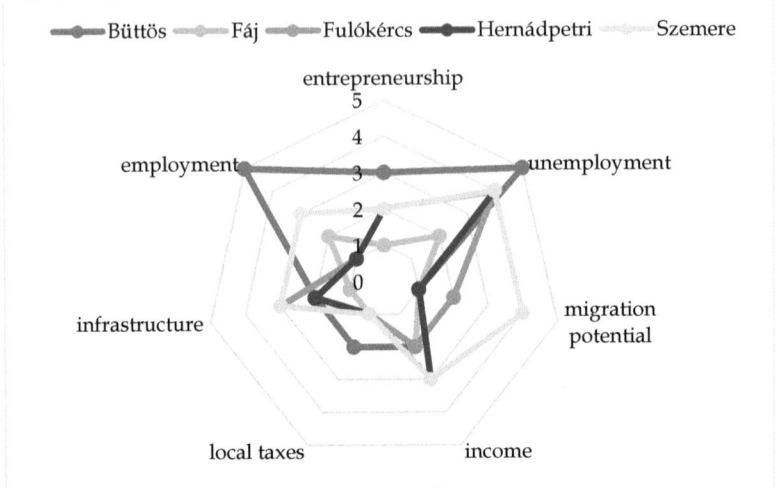

Figure 7: Economic potential
Source: the author

As we can see, only Büttös receives any local tax income — which is a common pattern in the region. Büttös tends to produce better results in terms of employment and unemployment as well (employment rate: 40,6%; unemployment rate: 4,5% in 2016). Several Slovakian citizens purchase properties in the village, they renovate houses which, in the future, may lead to a resort-like settlement. In terms of the economic potential, the data from Fáj is alarming. The lack of entrepreneurship, local taxes and modern infrastructure, together with high out-migration is very unsettling. In Fáj, the level of local knowledge and the number of higher education graduates are low, while local courage is non-existent.

Looking at the EP index (Figure 8), it is clear that Szemere and Büttös are in the most favourable position, followed by Fulókércs and Hernádpetri. Fáj ranks the lowest regarding this dimension as well.

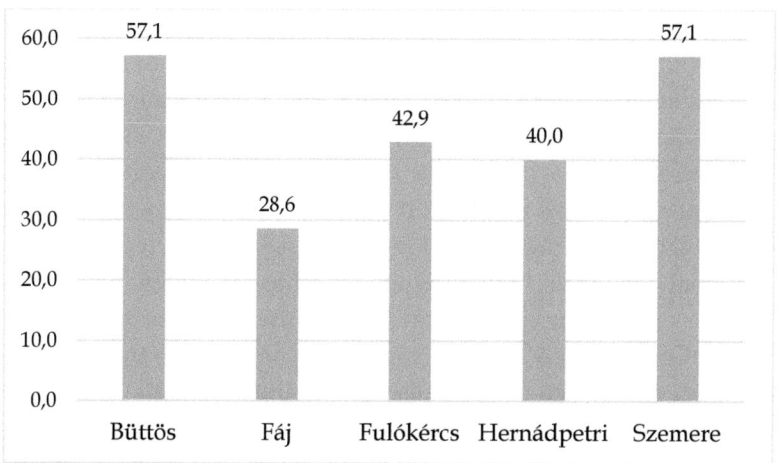

Figure 8: Economic potential index
Source: the author

The last pillar of the LIP index comes from the cultural and natural resources (CNR).

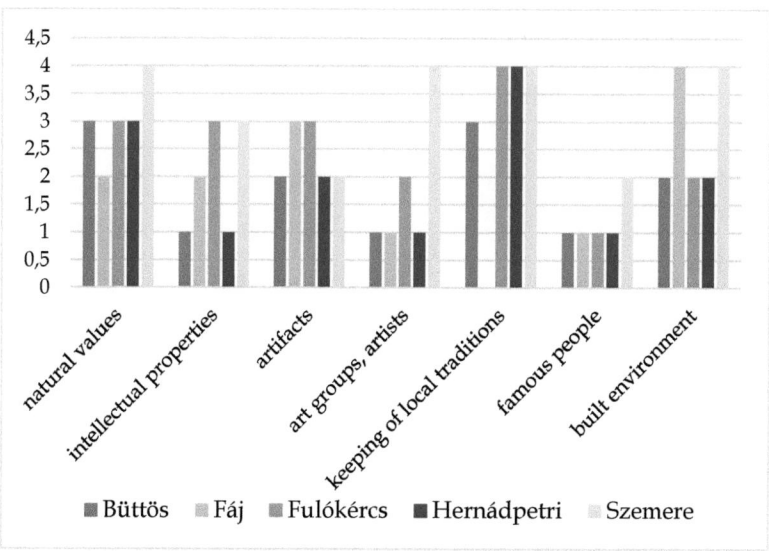

Figure 9: The items of the CNR index at the settlements
Source: the author

Figure 9 can show more elaborate correlations as well, underlining the popular belief that the inhabitants of Abaúj live in a beautiful natural environment but have a harsh life. A significant number of people keep local traditions, especially in Fulókércs, Hernádpetri and Szemere (in Fáj none of the interviewees could name any local traditions). In terms of the built environment, the Fáy mansion in Fáj (which, according to recent research has been removed from the National Castle and Forts Program) and the Pallavicini mansion in Szemere (that houses the local kindergarten) can be mentioned. Most of the artistic activity in Szemere is connected to the local elementary school, where specialised programmes in folk dance and arts are offered.

As illustrated by the figure above, Szemere had better results in the cultural and natural resources index than the other four settlements. Our qualitative research shows that the CNR index is high due to the mayor and a group of individuals being active in keeping the local traditions alive, encouraging artistic activities, organising local community events and working hard toward keeping the mansion and its park in good condition. The local government offers accommodation for travellers in the mansion of the former village clerk, Lajos Perlik.

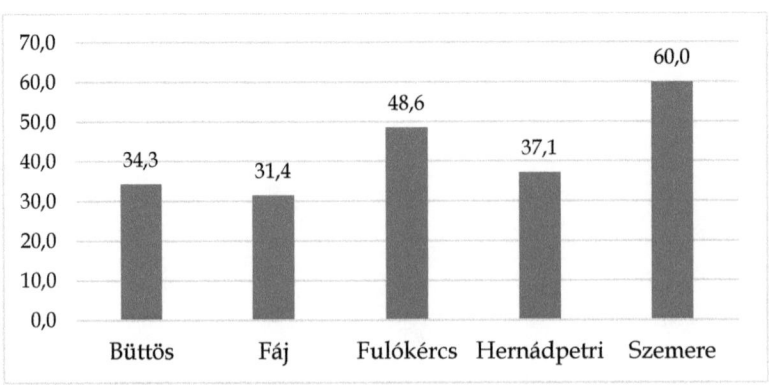

Figure 10: The values of the CNR index by settlements
Source: the authors

In relation to the CNR index (Figure 10), Fáj is the last one among the settlements in focus, while Szemere and Fulókércs are in a leading position.

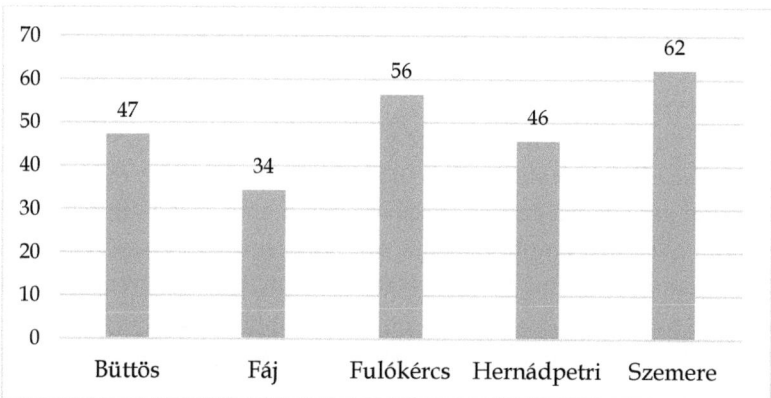

Figure 11: The values of local innovation potential by settlements (LIP)
Source: the author

Figure 11 shows the value of LIP at each settlement. Szemere has the highest local innovation potential, followed by Fulókércs and Büttös. Szemere got high points in all components used for the measurement of LIP, while Fáj received low points in all of them. Fulókércs is a leader in local courage – it is an outstanding community able to provide community well-being even if the economic conditions are unfavourable. Büttös and Hernádpetri are contradictory, which is clearly shown in their points for local innovation potential.

Summary

The study aimed to form an aggregated, integrated index based on the results of fieldwork and surveys capable of showing the local innovation potential and the possible ways of future developments. We also wanted to demonstrate that two settlements of a similar socio-demographic and geographical background can vary significantly, can show very different "patterns" and that two settlements that are very different at first glance (and at a second one as well) can face similar challenges and fall into one category.

In the future, we intend to test our index further, compare it to other indexes, broaden the research and "fine-tune" our index. As it is based on qualitative data, broadening the perspective has its limits (we cannot do research in thousands of settlements), but regional research is possible.

In our view, being an aggregated index containing small mosaics, the LIP index shows the colours, the similar patterns but also the existing shades and nuances of settlements. It is built on both qualitative and quantitative data, on "soft" and "hard" social scientific methods. It aims toward systematic analysis by creative and innovative approaches. It does not fail to mention that social realities and worlds depend on the point of view taken. They can only be shown from the perspective of parallel universes and opinions. The picture will never be homogenous or, at least, it will never be the same.

6.4. Social Innovation for Active Ageing

It is a truism that European countries are all ageing societies. It means that the proportion of elderly people (aged above 60) in the population is increasing and, concomitantly, the proportion of young people (aged 0-19) is decreasing. This process can also be seen in the stretched triangular shape of the age pyramid depicting the age and sex composition of the population. The advanced stage of the process is indicated by the fact that the number of young people is lower than the number of older people, even if the minimum demographic age limit for ageing is raised and the maximum age limit for young people is increased. Ageing is exacerbated by low fertility and migration, as well as the fact that there is an overall increase in average life expectancy at birth in European societies.

The World Health Organisation (WHO) adopted and started using the term "active ageing" in the late 1990s, with the purpose of giving ageing a positive connotation. The term "healthy ageing" may also be used but the former has several other dimensions. "Active ageing" denotes that the entire society can benefit from the knowledge, competencies and skills of the elderly. Furthermore, it suggests that, in addition to physical and mental well-being, social well-being is also important in old age, meaning that people in this age group should feel that they are an integral part of society and that they will not become invisible if they retire and do not participate in the labour market. At the same time, the concept of active ageing also implies striving to create a society where labour market participation is an option, not a constraint for older people. This would mean that they participate (whether full-time, part-time, teleworking, or other) not because it is an economic constraint, but because they have the opportunity and they wish to do so. In other words, the concept inherently involves the possibility of free choice for people to spend their years over 60 with activities that contribute to maintaining their quality of life and experiencing a happy, balanced old age. Active ageing also means that when they need it, they will be provided with proper protection, safety and care.

In addition, the adjective "active" implies equal treatment and opportunities, as well as both citizenship and labour market/economic participation. It also highlights that there should be a sense of interdependence and solidarity between generations.

Active ageing is an objective of several EU projects proposed in this area. In 2021, I had the opportunity to contribute to the implementation of a social innovation project on this topic as a professional manager. The present chapter reports on this work in the form of a case study.

The aim and framework of the project

The project "Active Ageing — Create a crossborder team of ambassadors in order to improve the quality of life for Slovak and Hungarian seniors" was submitted in the framework of the Interreg Hungary-Slovakia Cooperation Programme and implemented in 2021-2022. A Hungarian-Slovakian cooperation, the project was jointly developed by BORA 94 Borsod-Abaúj-Zemplén County Development Agency and Via Carpatia EGTC in Košice to support active ageing through improving the quality of life. The aim of the project was not only to create an Active Ageing Centre (a community space) in two locations (Miskolc and Košice) for inhabitants over 60 but to build on valuable senior knowledge and experience and promote the idea of volunteering among older people as well.

For long-term sustainability, the project outcome included designating senior ambassadors to become the driving force of the whole community, and sustain the community and the activities after the project, thus continuing community development among the target group. To achieve the above objectives, an internet platform called the Senior Platform was used, which not only enabled communication and information transfer but also became an interface for the "Circle of Favours" developed within the project. The latter provides an opportunity for each member of these age groups to offer their skills and services, and for others to take them or make offers themselves. In addition, a database of volunteer experts was set up, also with a view to long-term sustainability.

In order to disseminate good practices on active ageing, cross-border workshops were organised to exchange experiences and to involve Hungarian and Slovakian actors and professionals from organisations working with the elderly.

The rest of the chapter discusses how we identified and measured the over 60 age group, how we involved them in community activities, how we initiated volunteering among them, how the Active Ageing Centre and the online platform (with the Circle of Favours) were developed and how we could make the senior ambassadors continue the work we started.

Finding the target group, assessing their competencies and preparing their involvement

In the mid-summer of 2021, a questionnaire survey was carried out both online and offline as the basis of the programs offered by the Centre. Comprehensive needs assessment aimed to identify the lifestyle, activity and possible needs of the population over 60 in Miskolc and the county (the same was done in Košice), and to assess their competencies and their involvement in community building and volunteering.

The questionnaire was conducted online (mainly on Facebook and through a mailing list of organisations with elderly members) and in printed form.

The questionnaire measured the following dimensions:

1. the respondents' demographic background
2. their competencies, knowledge and skills
3. their willingness to volunteer
4. their activity, mental well-being and lifestyle
5. their social network, social capital and social activity
6. their willingness to participate in the planned activities of the Active Ageing Centre

The data were processed using SPSS Statistics software and published in a study. The original idea was to use the questionnaire as the basis for a voluntary network or a network of favours too. Eventually, it indirectly contributed to the former, as several people contacted us during the research and indicated their wish to join the project as volunteer experts, as well as to the latter, through the development of a knowledge pool.

The following questionnaire was used for the survey.

QUESTIONNAIRE
SKHU Ambassadors

Dear Respondent,

BORA 94 Borsod-Abaúj-Zemplén County Development Agency is conducting a survey among people aged 60 and over in the framework of its project "Active Ageing – Create a cross-border team of ambassadors in order to improve the quality of life for Slovak and Hungary seniors." The aim of the survey is to map the lifestyle, activity and possible needs of the population aged over 60 years in the county and in Miskolc.

Please help us implement the project by filling in the questionnaire below.

The questionnaire is anonymous and voluntary. The data will be used as summarised statistical results.

Dr. habil. Kinga Szabó-Tóth, Research Manager

---

1. Gender:
    1. male
    2. female

2. What year were you born?
    ....

3. What is your highest level of education? Select only one.
    1. less than 8 grades of primary school
    2. 8 grades of primary school
    3. vocational training
    4. secondary school diploma
    5. college or university degree

4. How many people live in your household? Select only one.
    1. I live alone
    2. two
    3. three

4. four
5. more than four

5. Your current economic status. Select only one.
   1. economically active, full-time job
   2. economically active, second job
   3. economically active, contract work
   4. economically inactive, stay-at-home parent
   5. economically inactive, retired
   6. retired and also working

6. What was your latest occupation?
   ....

7. Where do you live? Select only one.
   1. Miskolc
   2. another town in the county
   3. another municipality in the county

8. If you live in Miskolc, which part of the city do you live in? Select only one.
   1. Belváros, Avasalja, Vologda, Jókai, Mendikás
   2. Bodótető, Bábonyibérc, Tetemvár, Bedegvölgy
   3. Martin-kertváros, Szirma
   4. Görömböly, Hejőcsaba
   5. Szentpéteri kapu, Zsarnai, Repülőtér
   6. Selyemrét, Szondi, Csorba telep
   7. Népkert, Avas társasházi rész
   8. Avasi lakótelep
   9. Egyetemváros, Ruzsin
   10. Tapolca
   11. Komlóstető, Vargahegy
   12. Győri kapu
   13. Kilián, Békeszálló
   14. Lyukó
   15. Pereces
   16. Diósgyőr, Berekalja, Majláth
   17. Bükkszentlászló, Lillafüred, Ómassa, Jávorkút

9. How long have you lived in your current place of residence? Select only one.

1. since birth
2. since

10. Do you like living in the municipality? Select only one.
    1. yes
    2. no

11. Write three things you like best about the municipality where you live.
    ....
    ....
    ....

12. Name three things you dislike/least like about the place where you live.
    ....
    ....
    ....

13. How often do you spend your free time doing the following? Put an x in the relevant box.

	daily	weekly	monthly	yearly	a few times	never
watching television						
listening to the radio						
surfing the Internet						
doing sports						
fishing						
reading						
going to the theatre						
going to the cinema						
attending gatherings						
doing crafts						
gardening						
going on excursions						
walking						
travelling						

having
conversations
relaxing

14. Are you a member of a club, civil society organisation, sports club, other association or the Academy for Older People? Select only one.
   1.   yes: ....
   (name of the association, organisation or group)
   2. no

15. To what extent do you know the following? Please rate yourself (similarly to grades at school) from 1 to 5, with 1 being the lowest and 5 being the highest.
   speaking a foreign language
   finding information on the Internet
   doing DIY or crafts
   breeding animals
   growing plants
   dealing with money
   (e.g. insurance, stock exchange)
   running a business
   being with children, organising their free time
   participating in the work of civil society organisations
   dancing
   drawing, painting
   singing, playing a musical instrument
   keeping alive local traditions
   baking, cooking, canning

   BORA 94 Borsod-Abaúj-Zemplén County Development Agency is looking for active people aged 60 and over who would like to participate in carrying out activities that they have experience in and would like to practice on a regular or occasional basis.

16. Are there any activities or skills that you would like to participate in, that you would be willing to pass on to others, even in return for a fee? Select only one.

1. yes, for a fee (type of activity or knowledge):
....
2. yes, for free (the activity or type of knowledge):
....
3. none

17. Similarly, is there any activity or knowledge you would like to learn from others in the near future? Select only one.
   1. yes, for free:
   ....
   2. yes, for a fee:
   ....
   3. none

18. What communities do you attend and how often? Please put an x in the relevant box.

	daily	weekly	monthly	yearly	a few times	never
book club						
library						
dance group						
political party/group						
family gatherings						
a gathering of friends						
sporting events						

19. Describe yourself according to the following statements. Please rate yourself (similarly to grades at school) from 1 to 5, with 1 being the weakest and 5 being the strongest.
    I like to spend my time actively
    I like to help others in my free time
    I like being with animals and taking care of them
    I like being with children
    I like peace and quiet
    I like company
    I am generally optimistic, not afraid of the future
    I take the possible difficulties of ageing well
    I am not worried about my health
    I feel full of energy

I feel that I am in good health

20. Do you consider yourself a believer? Select only one.
    1. yes
    2. no

21. How often do you go to church? Select only one.
    1. every week
    2. only on holidays
    3. I no longer attend but used to
    4. I never attend, never have

22. Which city or county events do you know about or attend? Please put an x in the relevant box.

	know about	attend
Kocsonyfesztivál		
Avasi Borangolás		
Avasi Kvaterka		
Cinefest, Miskolc		
Miskolci régiségvásár		
Miskolci sörfesztivál		
Miskolc Város Napja-rendezvénysorozat		
Megyenap és rendezvényei		
Megyei vásárok (ónodi, csáti, egyebek)		
Harsányi Szürkemarha Fesztivál		
Falunapok		
Búcsúk		
Mádi Furmint Ünnep		
Zempléni Fesztivál		
Tarcali Bűbájos Hétvége		
Tokaj-Hegyalja Piac		
Operafesztivál		

23. Do you have any grandchildren? Select only one.
    1. yes
    2. no

24. If yes, where do they live? Select only one.
    1. in Miskolc
    2. in the county

3. in Budapest
4. elsewhere in Hungary
5. abroad

25. If yes, how regularly do you meet? Select only one.
    1. daily
    2. weekly
    3. monthly
    4. a few times a year
    5. never

BORA 94 Borsod-Abaúj-Zemplén County Development Agency, commissioning this survey, intends to establish a so-called Active Ageing Centre in Miskolc in September 2021 within the framework of a current tender. The centre plans to organise a variety of educational, health and sports programmes for residents aged 60 and over.

26. Would you attend the programmes and events organised by the centre? Select only one.
    1. yes
    2. no

27. Do you have any suggestions for activities or programmes that the centre could offer to residents over 60 in the fields of education, science, health or sport?
    no
    yes   (please   let   us   know):
    ....

Thank you very much for your answers!

If you would like to attend an event at the Active Ageing Centre, please read and complete the attached Privacy Policy.

The questionnaire was followed by the Privacy Policy, which described the purpose of data management and allowed the respondents to indicate whether they would like to receive information about the programmes and activities of the Active Ageing Centre in the future.

The Active Ageing Centre and its services

The centres are located in the city centres of Miskolc and Košice.

The services were designed to be adapted to the age and situation of the target group, and to maintain their physical and mental health and activity in the long term. The centre has a community space and machines for physical activity. When designing the services, we drew on the needs assessment of the primary target group and the activities they had proposed. The following programmes and events were organised:

- Science Without Borders — popular science lectures
- Art Space — art pedagogy workshops
- Activity — excursions, gymnastics, preserving physical activity
- Healthstore — promoting a healthy lifestyle
- Civic space — introduction of civil society organisations to promote the idea of volunteering
- Understanding — group activities to promote mental health
- Recipe Market — exchanging recipes and good food
- Games room — playing boardgames to stay mentally fit

The aim of offering these activities was to develop the community and facilitate their self-sustainment. The latter was achieved by involving the person who showed a willingness to do so in the questionnaire survey or during the individual sessions and discussions as a leader and by offering the opportunity to organise programmes and be active on online platforms. In this way, a group of 7 to 8 people was formed, whom we called senior ambassadors, i.e. ambassadors of the over 60 age group, who are also the driving force of the community.

At the last meeting led by us, we organised a full-day workshop on planning for the future. Working in small groups, the community members came up with ideas and then planned ways to implement them after the project was completed. At the end of the workshop, we asked them to create a Facebook group in a few days as a first step. The task was organised by a community member. When the Facebook page was set up, it had 30 members — a year later it had 300. Today (summer of 2024) the group has 665 members and is still growing. The community has become completely self-sustaining: they run the community space, scheduling opening and closing times and supervising it on a voluntary basis. They organise a variety of community activities, invite speakers, go on excursions, to the theatre, to the cinema, etc.

Developing the Senior Platform

At the time of the application, we contacted some relevant organisations (social institutions, institutions operating senior clubs, civil society organisations, etc.) which were involved as cooperating partners in the implementation and which, having day-to-day contact with the target group, are familiar with their needs, requirements and resources. They actively participated in ensuring that the Senior Platform, an online platform created to provide up-to-date information during the project and inform members of the target group about the services already available. We also contacted all the organisations working with and carrying out activities for the target group through the Internet and other sources. Their services were continuously added to those of our platform.

We also made available a database of volunteer experts and set up the Circle of Favours on the Platform, which will be discussed in the next two sections.

Creating the database of volunteer experts

When compiling the database of volunteer experts, we relied on our collaborating partners. Their accumulated knowledge and experience formed part of the database, and they provided the core team of experts.

Secondly, we reached out to potential volunteer experts both formally and informally through the online platform during the needs assessment. Informally, many of them indicated their willingness to join us in some way, and formally, they could indicate their intention to do so through the questionnaire, when asserting that they would like to receive information on the activities of the Active Ageing Centre.

These people were contacted again at the launch of the centre and informed about the possibility of joining the database of volunteer experts through a focus group interview and discussion.

Spreading the notion of volunteering was a priority during the implementation of the project, so we invited civil society organisations on several occasions and gave lectures on the methods and principles of volunteering.

As a result, the database was created with the participation of experts in the field of healthy living, legal advice, financial advice and security, among others. Our experts gave lectures and held workshops on a voluntary basis for the elderly, even after the project ended.

Establishing a circle or network of favours

As mentioned above, the Platform also includes a "Circle of Favours," through which the elderly population of the two counties can offer their help and skills to the community, individuals or any organisation. It also makes available the institutions, individuals, civil society organisations and businesses that welcome elderly people among their employees, either as volunteers or as paid workers. The Circle thus helps the elderly stay active, feel useful or join new communities.

Let me provide a little more detail about the Circle of Favours in general and the concept behind it.

The concept of a "circle of favours" — also known as a "favour bank," a "circle of exchange" or "kaláka kör" in Hungarian — is based on the idea that everyone has knowledge and skills that can help others.

In a circle of favours or exchanges, favours and 'indebtedness currency' are created and exchanged in the system, even without actual payment. In the simplest case, a platform is created where people with a wide range of competencies and skills find each other (virtually or otherwise) and can contact each other. Various needs and wishes can be written, formulated and asked for on the platform and, if the system is operational, there will be some kind of response to these wishes. The platform is based on the principle of reciprocity: everyone is good at something and even if "A" does not return the favour to "B" because "B" does not need that type of favour, the system works because "C" will be happy to receive that favour.

However, there is a significant drawback to the lack of monetary payment, which social scientists refer to as the "stowaway dilemma." In this case, the realisation of the common good is compromised by the fact that there are and always will be people — the stowaways and freeloaders — who do not contribute to maintaining the system but merely enjoy its benefits.

It is this problem that a circle of favours or exchanges eliminates by introducing an alternative form of currency, one with a symbolic value. It can be a voucher or a unit of time (time bank). The very essence of a favour bank is that members of a local community exchange favours among themselves, that is, they provide work or service, they give and take, and all this is accounted for by a value meter. As described earlier, the favours given and received by individuals must balance each other out in the long run, not between two individuals but at the level of the community. In other words, indirect barter can meet the diverse needs of the members and help avoid having a stowaway within the community. In a favour bank, the settlement of accounts thus takes the form of interest-free money, existing in a virtual form instead of a physical one or is exchanged as time invested in work (time bank). From "suska" to "fabatka" and "talentum," several names have been invented in Hungarian favour banks for this virtual measure of value. These virtual currencies facilitate exchange: we can not only provide each other with services but also offer each other products we have produced ourselves or objects and tools we no longer use, at appropriate prices. Experience has shown that to work well, a favour bank needs at least 50 and ideally a few hundred active members. The work requires forming a small group of organisers to make the organisation run more smoothly.

Whether called a circle of favours or a favour bank, it can have substantial benefits to society. It can help in reusing objects and expanding the market for local products. It can contribute to people's livelihoods, especially for those retired or excluded from the primary labour market. It can also have an important psychological impact by creating a sense of usefulness. It can operate on a completely voluntary basis and, as explained in detail above, as a form of 'paid' service.

The Circle of Favours Steps was developed through the following steps in the project:

- First, as part of the needs assessment, we created a knowledge pool based on who would provide what services or activities to others, either voluntarily or in return for payment. These were assessed thoroughly to provide a detailed insight into the competencies and strengths of the target group.
- Second, at the meetings of the Active Ageing Centre, we explained in detail the essence of the platform, thus building the online database and web interface.
- Third, the interface itself was and is still used as an opportunity for ongoing engagement.

Our platform for exchanging favours was fundamentally based on the notion of volunteering—an idea and practice which, as described above, we also promoted at the events of the Active Ageing Centre.

6.5. Promoting the Integration of People in Deprived Districts Through a Social Innovation Pilot Project

Slum, ghetto, tiny substandard flats. Former barracks and temporary shack housing. Irregular, forbidden, marginal, uncontrollable, spontaneous, unplanned, secretive and temporary. These are familiar phrases all over the world, even where the standards of living are generally higher and living conditions are better than average.

In several parts of the world, but especially in the European Union, there is a strong focus on improving the quality of life in deprived districts, disadvantaged neighbourhoods and lagging regions, as well as on promoting the inhabitants' social integration. Convergence regions are the most deprived ones in the EU; therefore, their development is a priority objective of the EU's regional policy.

The project VP/2020/003/0218 "Initiative for innovative integrated interventions in Miskolc - 4IM (Miskolc shall be a place for everyone) — A municipal initiative for innovative and integrated social services and employment development in Miskolc" was implemented between 2021-2024 with direct funding from Brussels as part of the Employment and Social Innovation Programme (EaSI). The project aimed to develop and implement an expandable model of integrated service provision that would ensure targeted coordination of social and employment services, focusing on two deprived districts of Miskolc, with continuous experience transfer with the city of Košice. The project was a social innovation pilot project using a range of innovative development tools, such as a model of integrated social service provision, developed to coordinate employment and social services, and community coaching (described in detail in an earlier chapter of this book), used for the involvement and empowerment of the population of the two districts.

In this case study, first I will briefly summarise the main objectives and results of the 4IM project, then provide a detailed description of the questionnaire survey carried out in two deprived districts, which served as the basis for the integrated service packages developed for the target group and set the course for possible social policy developments. The research conducted was innovative also because it was the first Hungarian adaptation of a model developed in the USA for segregated urban neighbourhoods.

Why is this model interesting? We believe that such a model-based typology is suitable for differentiated social policy support for the social integration of families living in deprived districts, highlighting the fact that people living in such areas do not form a homogeneous 'mass' but are characterised by various aspirations, motivations and cognitive patterns.

About the project and its results

The "Initiative for innovative integrated interventions in Miskolc - 4IM (Miskolc shall be a place for everyone) — A municipal initiative for innovative and integrated social services and employment development in Miskolc" was led by the Municipality of Miskolc, with the University of Miskolc, the Municipality of Košice, Association Européenne pour l'Information sur le Développement Loca (AEIDL), HÁRFA Foundation and Abaújrakezdés Association as consortium partners. I led the team at the University of Miskolc from 2001 to May 2023, which was responsible for the implementation of the research mentioned in the introduction.

The objective of the project was to introduce a new experimental social model, develop integrated interventions and institutional structures, and establish innovative cooperation among the organisations concerned in the public, municipal, civil and private sectors. The project envisaged that all these activities would contribute to the implementation of Principle 14 of the European Pillar of Social Rights: the introduction of a minimum income. A further aim was to set up a Social Innovation Resource Centre, which would work in coordination with various municipal departments (coordination, social affairs, press, communication and city marketing). In addition, local access points were planned to be set up in the two intervention areas: Tetemvár district and the segregated neighbourhood in Bábonyibérc district.

Under the proposal, the analyses for the development of the new service model were to be conducted by the University of Miskolc, the Municipality of Miskolc and the Abaújrakezdés Association, and coordinated by the Social Innovation Standing Working Group. The operational work was taken on by the Social Innovation Resource Centre, with the aim of managing an integrated (pilot) scheme to support the poorest households. Implementing the pilot model was the task of the local access points in Tetemvár and Bábonyibérc.

A further objective was for Miskolc to share its experience with its partner city, Košice and to join the work of European municipal networks cooperating in similar projects (8 successful applications with similar objectives from countries such as Germany, Italy, France and Slovakia).

The project had several expected outcomes: (1) a more efficient and integrated model of social and employment services in Miskolc, consciously developed and pilot-tested at a municipal level; (2) an adaptable, scalable model that could be used for other segregated areas; (3) Miskolc's participation in European knowledge-sharing networks, becoming known and finding partners to facilitate moving forward; (4) better access to services for the inhabitants of the segregated district, reducing disparities and aiding social mobility; and (5) if the pilot model could be operated in Miskolc, the Resource Centre would continue work in the long term after the project was completed, with further deprived neighbourhoods added to the access points.

The planned objectives and the new innovative model-concept were to be implemented through the following activities:

- Reviewing the social situation and the functioning and effectiveness of relevant local policies, regulations, services and institutions
- Setting up a Social Innovation Standing Working Group
- A household-level survey in Tetemvár and Bábonyibérc
- Setting up a Social Innovation Resource Centre
- Capacity-building workshops for those involved in project implementation

- Implementation of a community coaching process to activate and involve the target group in the two target areas
- Establishment of community working groups in Tetemvár and Bábonyibérc
- International study tours to visit similar EaSI projects
- Establishment of a municipal-level action plan to promote the social (and territorial) integration of deprived districts
- Setting up local access points in the two districts
- Setting up and implementing an integrated model of social and employment services and financial support
- Testing the new service package in Bábonyibérc and Tetemvár, with the participation of at least 300 individuals
- Continuous experience transfer with the city of Košice

The project closure report presents the results achieved as follows (Márczis—Scharle—Török, 2024: 7-8):

"Briefly, in line with the objectives of the 4IM project at a municipal level:

- Cooperation among actors has been established, strengthened and institutionalised; inter-organisational and inter-personal relationships have increased significantly, and a need for cooperation and the structure thereof has been established, ensuring the continuation of joint work after the end of the project.
- An innovative integrated service model, including the integration of employment services and the institutional model, has been developed and briefly tested in Miskolc.
- Household-level mapping and connecting, the application of the individual life-course plan method and individual follow-up have been enabled and developed.
- Social participation in local decision-making.
- Miskolc has a plan on how to continue the integration of deprived districts step-by-step.
- In the selected deprived districts, Bábonyibérc and Tetemvár, the more than three hundred inhabitants participating

- got closer to entering the labour market, those close to being employed at the beginning of the intervention participated in training or other activation activities,
- were brought closer to other services that facilitate integration,
- were involved as active partners in the development of services and became participants in local decision-making.

The methodology applied during and the lessons learnt from the implementation of the sustainable and replicable tools of the 4IM project:

- Though hardly visible due to the short timeframe and the difficult problems, the living conditions have started to improve.
- Access to local employment and social services has improved.
- The residents made active have had the experience of how the action they take can improve their living conditions.
- In terms of extension and sustainability:
- The new service system is extended to other neighbourhoods in the city and adaptation has started in the partner city, Košice, Slovakia.
- Miskolc has begun its integration into the network of similar municipal initiatives, as meetings organised by EaSI on similar projects and study visits to the German and Tuscan sister projects have raised awareness and created new contacts that could be beneficial in the future."

The research and its innovative results

As highlighted earlier, the aim of the research was to map households and individuals in the two target areas and serve as the basis of the integrated service packages designed for the target group. The innovativeness of the study lay in adapting John R. Seeley's concept of segregation in US metropolises. The typology resulting from this adaptation proved to be entirely applicable to setting the guidelines of the social policy interventions aimed at the target group.

The theoretical framework of the research — the sociological characteristics of segregated urban neighbourhoods

According to Antal Bőhm (1992), the deepening of the socio-economic crisis creates spatially well-defined ease to locate "depression zones." This leads to the emergence of certain territorial units, enclaves, which are predominantly characterised by infrastructural deficits or intellectual and cultural deprivation and unemployment.

In 1929, Jahoda et al. described four coping strategies used by groups facing long-lasting crises. The first group is called the "unbroken". People in this category have a vision of the future, (so) they are constantly looking for work, they keep their households in order, and the children are neat. The second type is the "resigned." They are characterised by a lack of plans, a lack of vision and living from hand to mouth. They accept their situation and reduce their needs accordingly. They expect nothing from life, they are calm and enjoy the small pleasures of life. They take care of their children. The third type, those "in despair," are characteristically desperate and depressed. They live in the past, no longer look for work but look after their children. Fourthly, "the apathetic" are characterised by irrational management, which means immediately spending the benefits, a family in ruins and addictions.

People in particularly difficult situations may develop what theoretical literature calls a "present-oriented habitus" (e.g. Stewart, 2001; Ladányi—Szelényi, 2004), characterised by the inability to delay gratification, and by a lack of ability and need to plan for the longer term.

In Castel's theory (2000), people living in extreme poverty are a "disaffiliated social group," for whom deprivation may even result in extreme insecurity and a decline in cognitive abilities (Szabó-Tóth 2004; 2005).

Regarding urban slums, one crucial question that arises is how their inhabitants could be characterised in terms of social and systemic integration. Social integration pertains to the family and, by extension, the kinship network, the living environment, the neighbourhood and friendships. Systemic integration is connected to acquiring community norms and customs, with various social institutions and organisations as the primary settings. If a community is spatially and/or socially segregated, this can lead to the emergence of "small community life-worlds" with their own set of norms and values, in which systemic integration is impaired.

The typification of urban slums is a vital aspect thereof. It can be done based on their physical and social characteristics.

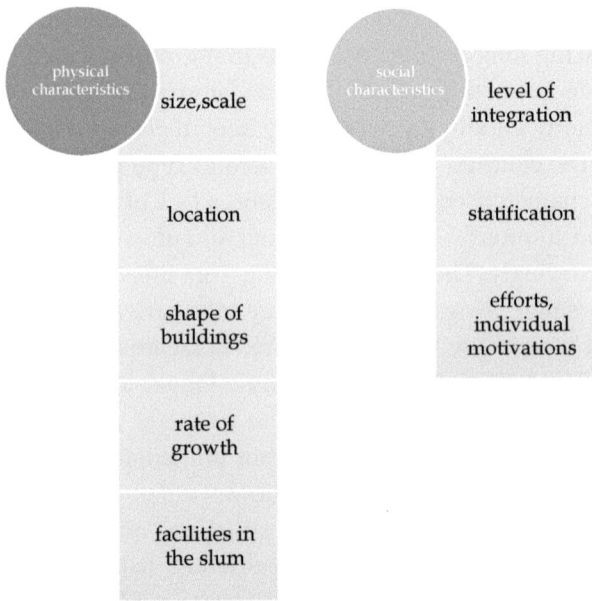

Figure 1: Typology of urban slums
Source: own editing

The essential distinction between an urban slum and a segregated rural area is that the former serves as a first mobilisation 'channel' for the inhabitants, that is, a stepping stone for those moving to cities from rural areas enabling adaptation to urban life. This is a significant difference between the two.

A 2010 study (Teller, 2011) found that the most common reasons for moving to an urban slum are escaping the high maintenance costs of the previous dwelling, the importance of kinship ties and founding a family. In comparison, the reasons for moving out are employment, studies, escaping a poor environment and housing conditions, and becoming independent. The latter are more likely to lead to upward mobility (Havasi, 2018).

A major factor in moving to or leaving the slum, and slum life as such, is people's network of relationships, their strong and weak ties. These ties can, on the one hand, draw them to the slum (from the village towards urban life) and, on the other, be a 'pull' later (out of the slum and towards non-slum forms of urban life). The significance of these leverage effects will be described in detail when presenting the results, as well as in the summary section, as they are regarded as key elements of our research and the concomitant interventions.

Regardless of which above dimension is examined and what the results are, urban slums have certain features in common, in addition to those mentioned and highlighted above: there is a high proportion of younger age groups, high population density, high morbidity and mortality rates, low levels of health care and education, low and irregular incomes, and concentrated deviance. They may also be characterised by serious religious and ethnic conflicts, as well as having reserves of strength, a tendency for self-organisation, and being resourceful when money-making.

The urban slum as a phenomenon cannot be eliminated from urban life, most importantly because it has certain socio-economic functions for both its inhabitants and the environment (the local population and city leaders), such as adaptation and protection, integration (creating its own order and rules, spontaneous development regulated by the inhabitants), solidarity, capitalisation (the often illegally built public utilities are legalised over time).

The inhabitants of urban slums are not a homogeneous block—they may differ in a wide range of social and individual characteristics. The following typology can be used to classify slum dwellers along two parameters: whether they view the place as a necessity or an opportunity, as permanent or temporary.

	Need/destitution	Opportunity/opportunists
perma-nent	1. The apathetic: They resigned themselves to living permanently in the district and are depressed or depression-prone. They lost their motivation. They are often alcoholics or addicts. They have been out of work for years and do not take care of their children. They may be in state care. Their home is in a neglected state. They are on the edge of existence. They are apathetic and immobile. It is quite unlikely that they will ever leave the district. 2. The resigned poor: They have come to terms with their situation. They live in deprivation and destitution. They obey the law and adjust to the slum and the world outside. They do not protest against their situation. They take care of their children and grandchildren. They may starve by the end of the month as they have few resources to live on. They may have some income, such as disability annuity. Drinking and other deviances are uncommon in this group. They enjoy their independence and are usually unwilling to leave the district for a little comfort elsewhere. Many of them are elderly or single women with children. They do not have the money to leave and	6. The fugitives: People running away from the law or a credit institution. The district is a refuge for them. 7. The untraceable: They have no identity or cannot be identified; they are invisible to society. They cannot fit into society and are extreme individualists. The society has no room for them. 8. The role models: They are gurus, great old ones, wise men. They tell others how things are, they know their drill. They know and shape local rules and act as informal leaders. 9. The athletes: They are eccentrics who enjoy living in the district. They are often feared by others because of their erratic behaviour. They like to get into trouble and form gangs. They like the district because of the low cost of living and being able to spend their money on other things.

	often also lack the motivation to do so. 3. The outcasts of society: They are disaffiliated from society and have often been excluded by society itself. They cannot move away from the district, primarily because the majority is not interested in them. They have settled in the district. In most cases, they are involved in illegal activities, they are often prostitutes, pimps or drug addicts. They feel comfortable in the district because at least they have a sense of belonging.	
temporary	4. The struggling poor: They have lived outside the district throughout their lives but now live here for the most part. They are similar to the resigned poor, except for having an identity and most of their relationships outside the slum. They can break out with help, for example, if someone buys their house and offers them social housing in another part of the city. They pay their bills and obey the majority rules. 5. The trapped: They moved here when the district was in a better state and they cannot move away because their home is worthless. They can also be helped, for instance with a prepaid	10. The beginners: They have moved here from the countryside and they do not fit in or know anyone. They live here temporarily and do not want to stay. They get acquainted with city life and then move on as soon as they can. This group predominantly consists of families with young children, intent to learn how to live in a city and become a parent. They move on when they can, unless more children are born, which ties them to the district. 11. The climbers: They are similar to the beginners but have lived longer in the district and want to save enough money to leave. They have savings. They are

	electricity meter card or a renovation.	hard-working. They are often homeowners and diligent savers. 12. The entrepreneurs: They are even more ambitious than the climbers. They have a small shop or business in the slum. Usually at around the age of 50, they move away from the district to a better one.

Figure 2: Typology of the inhabitants of urban slums
Source: Seeley, 1959

Contributions to a better understanding of the target areas in Miskolc

Taking a historical perspective and tracing the changes in the population of Miskolc shows that the population tripled in the 19th century (Lengyel, 2009). In terms of the Roma population, the 1767 census registered 35 adults and 41 children in 17 families, while according to the 1837 census, there were 32 Roma families with 106 members. At the end of the 19th century, the census recorded 372 Roma people dwelling or staying in Miskolc (Lengyel, 2009).

Figure 3: Poor settlements and Roma slums in Miskolc and Diósgyőr in the 19th and 20th centuries
Source: Lengyel, 2009.

At the beginning of the 20th century, there was a great demand for labourers, servants and day labourers, owing to the state-owned ironworks and the mine in Pereces. The permanent workers lived in colonies (established, in part, with the help of the city), while the temporary workers lived in the urban slums (Lengyel, 2009). These included the so-called "Numbered Streets" built by the ironworks, which were of poorer quality than those built for the inner areas of the plant. Similar dwelling places were also built near the lime works in Hejőcsaba and the quarry in Miskolcapolca (Lengyel, 2009). The narrow courtyards, nooks and corners of the inner area were inhabited by day labourers, seasonal workers and servants in small tenement houses.

On the edge of the rows of cellars in Tetemvár, near the boneyard, a new slum called Honfoglaló formed between the two world wars. It was inhabited by the most deprived group, the destitute and the evicted, in small huts they built themselves (Lengyel, 2009).

The Gordon and Szonditelep neighbourhoods were the largest slums in Miskolc between the two world wars. The latter was transformed from a hospital and wards built next to the barracks of the Szonditelep artillery regiment for the city's poor, and in time the wooden barrack-like buildings were rebuilt in stone. From 1974, Roma families were moved here from their dwellings on the bank of the River Sajó (called Csorbatelep back then) after the flood, and when the Gordon slum was eliminated, its inhabitants were likewise moved here. With time, the population of the neighbourhood transformed: the Roma families moved out to live in better conditions, the houses deteriorated and most of the inhabitants became unemployed. In 1992 a decision was drawn up for a slum clearance, but no radical change took place until 2008, when the majority of the houses were demolished, the land increased in value and was sold. The residents were moved to the remaining slums in the city (the Numbered Streets, Miskolctapolca Quarry and some to the Avas district, as part of the Nest Programme). Approximately 20 or 25 flats were still inhabited in unsettled circumstances. At the beginning of the 2000s, with the help of the Roma minority self-government, comfortable terraced houses with 18 flats and a larger apartment block containing 24 social rental apartments were built on the south-eastern side of the neighbourhood.

After the Second World War, heavy industry development increasingly attracted to the city both unskilled and skilled workers, often former peasants, who could find their homes in the newly built housing estates. As part of this building boom, the Honfoglaló and Gordon slums were demolished (the latter was replaced by the Vörösmarty housing estate). From the 1980s on, more advantaged social groups started to move into the suburbs and the demand for large inner-city housing increased (Lengyel, 2009).

The hostel Békeszálló was built in the late 1940s and was originally intended to be a temporary accommodation for workers (Lengyel, 2009). It contained one-bedroom apartments and was first inhabited by settled workers, then, when they found better housing (workers of LKM and Digép), Roma families were moved into the empty flats after the elimination of the slum. By the end of the 1980s, the better-off Gypsy families also left the settlement, and only those living in the worst conditions remained. In the decade before the regime change, it became another large Roma slum besides Szonditelep.

The inhabitants of the Tatárdomb and Erdőalja settlements were also continually evicted, first to the old houses on the main street in Diósgyőr, then, from the late 1980s, to the Numbered Streets and the mining colonies of Pereces.

The residents of Csorbatelep were badly affected by the flood of 1974. Some of the families were moved to the Szonditelep slum (as mentioned earlier), to backyards and larger flats in the city centre, and the dilapidated houses near the market on Búza Square. Furthermore, abandoned military buildings were also used for such purposes: for instance Álmos Yard, with 15 families moving in from Csorbatelep.

In the 1970s and 1980s, the number of Roma inhabitants also increased. Research conducted by Pál Tóth in 1987 indicated that Roma people made up 5 % of the population, that is, approximately 10-12 thousand people. These families came from villages in the county and migrated to the city in the hope of a better life (i.e. relatively adequate housing and employment). As a result of the housing policy, which supported families with many children, some Roma families could move to the housing estates in the Avas district.

Partly due to the growing number of the Roma population and partly to the fact that some families were moved to the main street, the mid-1980s saw a growing anti-Roma sentiment in the city. In order to resolve the situation (and to vacate the large flats in the city centre), the city council came up with a plan to resettle these families back to the banks of the River Sajó. The plan was to build four small flats without one building, with a water tap on the street. In 1989, local intellectuals and Roma inhabitants, joined by intellectuals from the capital, prevented the implementation of the plan.

After the regime change, several plans were drawn up to demolish socially deprived residential areas in the city. As a result, the eviction of Roma inhabitants from the main street began, followed by the elimination of the slums in Pereces, Szonditelep and Békeszálló. The terraced houses of Mésztelep were also evicted.

Several people moved to the Numbered Streets, the industrial monument site of the former and the lower part of Tetemvár.

In the past 20 years, Roma inhabitants have moved into wine cellars and wine houses used as residential buildings, as well as privately-owned, small, delipidated houses, predominantly in certain areas of Bábonyibérc and Tetemvár.

Meanwhile, a new slum emerged in Lyukóvölgy, an underdeveloped neighbourhood on the outskirts of Miskolc. In the 1970s and 1980s, the area was used as a weekend retreat by workers LKM, and several families moved here from the late 1980s on, having sold their flats in the city (usually in panel buildings). In the first decade after the regime change, poorer families started to move to Lyukóvölgy, buying cheap houses built of wood or stone. Many bought plots to build a house on at a low cost. Roma families began to move here in the following decades, especially from the early 2000s on (we shall not look into the Lyukóvölgy settlement in detail here).

In 2008, the Municipality of Miskolc prepared an anti-segregation plan for its urban slums as part of the Integrated Urban Development Strategy (hereinafter ITS) completed in 2014 and 2018.

According to the 2011 census data, 2,470 people lived in segregated areas in the inner city and 2,481 people on the outskirts of Miskolc (in Lyukóbánya and Lyukóvölgy). According to these data, the most populated inner area slums were the Numbered Streets, Szondi Street, Tetemvár and the neighbourhood of Békeszálló.

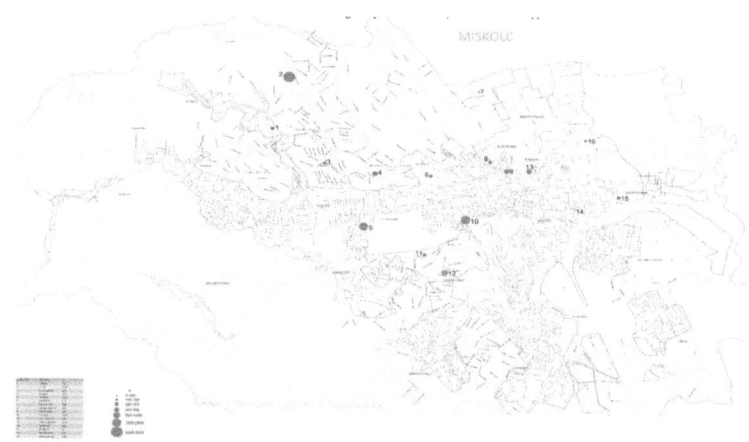

Figure 4. The deprived districts of Miskolc
Source: Analysis by the Working Group for the Integration of Deprived Districts, 2021.

In 2021, the Working Group for the Integration of Deprived Districts identified 16 such districts, including Lyukóvölgy, as well as two new emerging slums, Rózsás dűlő and Csermőke dűlő.

The segregated neighbourhood of Bábonyibérc was defined to be delimited by both sides of the new settlement in Bábonyibérc, Bábonyibérc sor, Bábonyibérc felső sor, Tinódi Street and Feszty Árpád Street, while the Tetemvár slum was delimited by Belterületi határ, Tetemvár középsor, Tetemvár alsósor, Arany János Square, Laborfalvi Róza Street, Temető Street and the dirt road.

The report made by the Working Group for the Integration of Deprived Districts characterised the Tetemvár district in the following way: It has 500 inhabitants. 40% of the inhabitants live in extreme poverty. 90% of the inhabitants are Roma. The rate of children at risk is 67% in the 0-3 age group, 25% for children aged 3-6 years, and 50% for children of compulsory school age. The dropout rate among children living in the slum is 85%. 20% of the economically active population has a job. There are 2-3 families who may be regarded as squatters. Most households have electricity but no piped water, sewage or central gas heating. They heat with wood. Water is obtained from a nearby communal well. The average family size is 4-5 persons.

Based on the same report, the characterisation of Bábonyibérc is as follows: A steadily growing slum with 450 inhabitants, 80% of whom live in extreme poverty. 80% of the inhabitants are Roma. 70% of children under the age of 6 and 75% of school-age children are at risk. The school drop-out rate is 10%. 40% of the working-age population are unemployed. The average family size is 5-8 persons. Most households have electricity but no piped water, sewage or gas. Refuse collection is provided.

Research methodology

The survey carried out and presented here covered the population of the target areas of Bábonyibérc (both sides of the new settlement in Bábonyibérc, Bábonyibérc sor, Bábonyibérc felső sor, Alsó sor, Galagonyás sor) and Tetemvár (Tetemvár felső sor, Tetemvár középsor, Tetemvár alsósor). The basic unit of observation was the household, while the unit of analysis was the individual, the household, the community and the district.

The research was based on a questionnaire survey, since our aim was to contact all households and create a database recording the relevant parameters of the families. The research measured attitudes, dispositions and opinions, and used households as sources of information.

Our investigation was conducted in three main problem areas (dimensions):

- Socio-demographic circumstances (composition of the household, education, employment, housing, children, health, deviances)
- Attachment and motivations (weak and strong ties within and outside the settlement, connections and embeddedness, local attachment and involvement in local affairs)
- Resources (financial, material, psychological, social, as well as existing competencies of the population)

The survey was conducted through intensive and extensive research based on three questionnaires: a household survey questionnaire, a personal questionnaire and a data sheet for each individual of a household aged 16 and over. The questionnaire was based on the UNDP Regional Bureau for Europe and the Commonwealth of Independent States (RBEC) household-based survey questionnaire used in Cluj-Napoca, Brăila and Pécs.

The questionnaire data were gathered with the help of interviewers between 14 June and 5 August 2022. It was preceded by the training of the interviewers and a site visit to identify the streets and neighbourhoods with the help of the staff of the Social Innovation Resource Centre. During the questionnaire survey, each interviewer covered an area of approximately 25 plots of land with land register reference. On average, one questionnaire took about 1-1.5 hours to fill (in some cases it was 30 minutes, other times several hours).

A diagnosis of the settlements — key research findings[9]

Socio-demographic circumstances (composition of the household, education, employment, housing, children, health, deviances)

The segregated district of Tetemvár (Tetemvár felső sor, középső sor, alsó sor and Tetemvár sor) is an area close to the city centre with a socially mixed population (which shall be discussed in detail later). Being within a mere 5-minute walking distance from the centre, it is also important from a strategic aspect for the city. The Hungarian Charity Service of the Order of Malta operates its Presence Programme in the neighbourhood. The area examined has several cellars and wine houses. Most of the houses are unfurnished, with little or no comfort, or emergency shelters, but there are also larger houses with several rooms and neat little houses. In many cases, the inhabitants live here based on informal contracts and other forms of unresolved property ownership. There are a number of illegal

---

[9] The research results were extracted from the SPSS database and the graphs were created in cooperation with Helga Mihályi.

waste sites in the area which is full of rats, according to the residents.

Based on our surveys, we registered 107 occupied properties (it must be noted, though, that some are in such a poor condition that they could collapse at any time in which case they will be quickly demolished—therefore, the number of houses varies greatly). Unoccupied properties or uninhabitable dilapidated unoccupied houses: 59. No existing address or plot: 62. In the area delineated, an estimated maximum of 350 people live currently.

We were able to survey 55 of the 107 properties, which meant gathering information on 165 individuals altogether. 39 households refused to respond and members of 13 households were away from the house at each repeated visit (so it is not known whether these are actually occupied properties).

Picture 1: A dilapidated cellar in Tetemvár
Source: own photo

In the segregated area of Bábonyibérc (both sides of the new settlement, Bábonyibérc sor, Bábonyibérc felső sor, Alsó sor, Galagonyás sor) 200 plots were registered. 86 of them were inhabited and 49 households were successfully queried. Of the 200 plots, 37 are unoccupied properties, 43 properties do not exist or have been demolished, and 34 properties were cellars or wine cellars. We gathered detailed information on about 172 of the estimated 300 individuals living in the district. The segregated area has a steadily increasing population, including both Roma and non-Roma inhabitants. Few households have access to gas and water, and several families obtain water from communal wells. In many households, there is no sewage disposal, so domestic sewage flows into the street. The area also has rodents and a lot of rubbish in certain places.

Picture 2. A waste site in Bábonyibérc
Source: own photo

Picture 3: The organised part of Bábonyibérc
Source: own work

The two areas are similar in some characteristics. Approximately seven-thirds of the residents moved to the area before 2000. The proportion of new settlers in Bábonyibérc was particularly high in the first decade of the 2000s, while the same was true for Tetemvár after 2010.

The latter phenomenon was largely due to the elimination of the segregated area of Álmos Street, as well as some inhabitants of the Numbered Streets moving here. 77% of the residents of Tetemvár and 83% of those of Bábonyibérc were born in Miskolc.

The ethnic composition of the two areas is also quite similar (based on the self-identification of the respondents): one-quarter of the residents identify themselves as Roma.

In terms of age composition, a greater proportion of the inhabitants is elderly in Tetemvár than in the other target area, as reflected in the following rates: the share of people living alone due to widowhood is 20% and 10% in Bábonyibérc. The proportion of married people is 60% in Tetemvár and 75% in Bábonyibérc. From the aspect of educational attainment, the proportion of people who have 8 years of schooling or less is 50% in Tetemvár and 45% in Bábonyibérc.

Figure 5: The economic activity of respondents
Source: own research

The employment figures are significantly higher in Tetemvár: more than half of the respondents are employed, approximately one in ten are unemployed and only 3.7% do not work for other reasons. At the same time, it is also clear that nearly 31% of the residents of Tetemvár are pensioners; that is, as reckoned, the area is predominantly inhabited by an older age group.

The economic activity indicators of the inhabitants living in the part of the Bábonyibérc delimited and studied, are rather unfavourable. The employment rate is 39%, while the unemployment rate is 18.4%. The proportion of people who do not work for other reasons (e.g. staying at home as a housewife or with children, due to illness or a disability) is likewise high, 18.4%.

As a community, Bábonyibérc is characterised by a young population and households with several children. The rate of families with 5 or more children is 22.4%, and 7.3% in Tetemvár. In 56% of households in Tetemvár, there are no young people under 16, compared to 47% in Bábonyibérc. The proportion of single-person households — mainly elderly single women — is 22% in Tetemvár and 16% in Bábonyibérc.

In both segregated areas, nearly 80% of the residents live in their own real estate. According to the respondents, 8% of the residents of Tetemvár and 3% of the inhabitants of Bábonyibérc get an eviction note at some point during their stay. Running water is available in 72% of the households in Tetemvár and in 61% of the properties in Bábonyibérc. 18% of residents of Tetemvár and 37% of those living in Bábonyibérc obtain water from a communal well, and only one-half of the former and one-third of the latter have piped gas.

Based on the responses, 10% of the inhabitants of Tetemvár and 20% of those in Bábonyibérc had a period in their lives when they could not heat their home at all, while 5% of the former and 15% of the latter reported that the family went to bed hungry because they could not afford to buy food.

Since the families surveyed had moved to these segregated areas, one-fourth of the properties suffered minor damage due to storms or leaking. It is somewhat troubling that one-fifth of the families reported their house damaged by another resident of the neighbourhood. The data on major snow or ice damage shows considerable differences between the two areas studied: the figure is 5.5% in Tetemvár and 16.3% in Bábonyibérc.

Attachment and motivations
(weak and strong ties within and outside the settlement, connections and embeddedness, local attachment and involvement in local affairs)

Just over half of the inhabitants of Tetemvár and 44% of those living in Bábonyibérc are dissatisfied with their living environment. It comes as no surprise that, as illustrated by Figure 7, on a scale of one to ten, the overall sense of safety in the two neighbourhoods was rated 4.8 (the figure is lower in Bábonyibérc than in Tetemvár). Yet, it is indeed surprising that the answers to the question of how much the residents like living there were more favourable (6 for Tetemvár, and 5.7 for Bábonyibérc on a scale of one to ten).

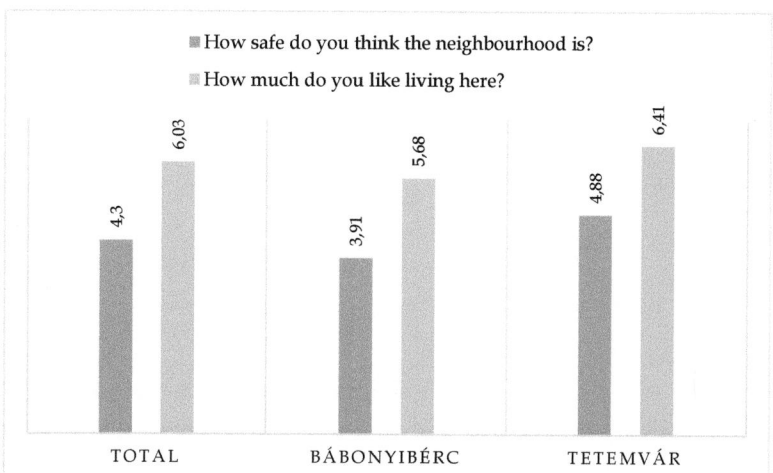

Figure 6: A sense of safety and attachment to the place — in a ten-point scale
Source: own research

Although the feeling of safety and attachment to the neighbourhood was rated lower by the residents of Bábonyibérc than those of Tetemvár, the rate of people who indicated they had no plans to move away in the near future was higher for the former than the latter.

Attachment to place was also measured by how active the respondents were in local affairs, whether they did something for their place of residence, helped organise local events, and so on.

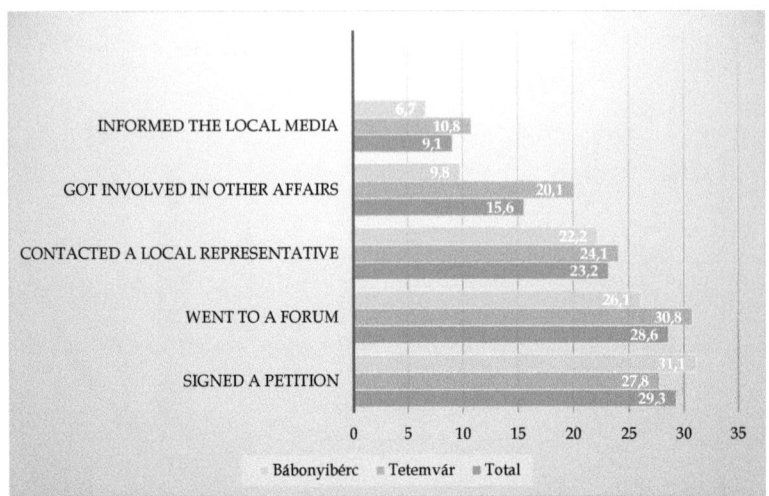

Figure 7: Activity in local affairs
Source: own research

Figure 7 shows a relatively high level of active involvement among the residents of both districts, with one in four or five people going to forums, signing a petition or contacting their local representative.

During the period of the questionnaire survey (the summer of 2022), community development programmes had already been launched as part of the project in both areas but mainly in Bábonyibérc; thus, its residents there showed more activity on a weekly basis than the inhabitants of Tetemvár. Furthermore, the data series also indicates that the latter had a higher level of community activity in the past, presumably owing to the Presence Programme of the Order of Malta operating in the neighbourhood.

In addition to attachment to the place, weak and strong ties were also measured by two questions in the questionnaire: first, whether there was someone to look after their children when they were absent and if so, did they live in the neighbourhood or elsewhere, and second, who they could borrow money from.

Answers to the first question reveal a high level of embeddedness, as several people leave their children in the care of relatives or neighbours in the settlement if they need to. Such an attachment reinforces and demonstrates a local identity tied to the neighbourhood. Strong or weak ties connecting people outward, that is, the existence of so-called identification points outside the district, are important indications of one not being completely trapped in the settlement.

The second question—who you could borrow money from if you were financially strapped—is likewise an important indicator. Based on the answers, one in five people can indeed ask for help with such matters, while in Bábonyibérc one in four would prefer to turn to relatives in the settlement in case of financial hardship, which indicates a fairly high level of cooperation.

Regarding the place of residence of the person who could lend them money, results suggest that people in Tetemvár are more likely to have ties with people outside the neighbourhood, that is, they have weak or strong ties connecting them outward.

Another question inquired who the inhabitants would turn to for help in case of trouble and where this person lives. Here, too, the answers clearly indicate that one in two people from Tetemvár would prefer to turn to someone from outside the neighbourhood who does not live in a segregated area but another part of Miskolc.

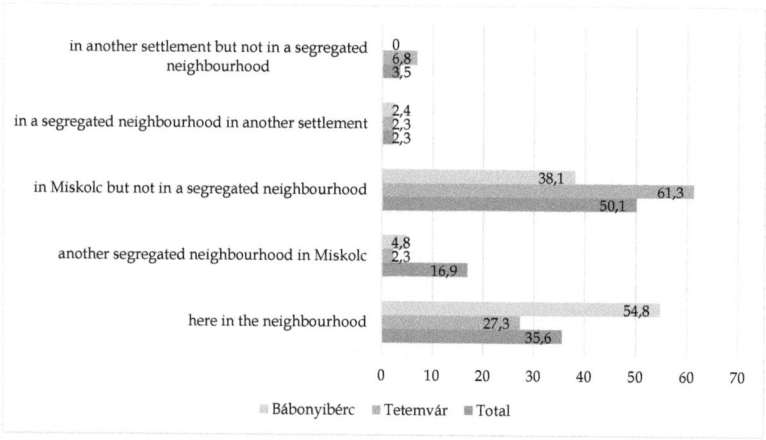

Figure 8: Where does the person you could turn to in case of trouble live?

Source: own research

	Total	Tetemvár	Bábonyibérc
here in the neighbourhood	40,9	35,5	50,0
another segregated neighbourhood in Miskolc	12,2	12,9	11,1
in Miskolc but not in a segregated neighbourhood	30,6	35,3	22,2
in a segregated neighbourhood in another settlement	6,1	6,4	5,6
in another settlement but not in a segregated neighbourhood	10,2	9,7	11,1
Total	100,0	100,0	100,0

Table 1: Where do your closest friends live?

Source: own research

The table above indicates that Bábonyibérc is a more integrated and cohesive community, with one in two people replying that their closest friends live in the settlement. The data also show that, as in the case of several other questions, Tetemvár is better connected to the city, both geographically and in other ways, since one in three people have their closest friends in Miskolc but not in the neighbourhood.

Local embeddedness and attachment were also investigated by asking respondents what they regard as the most urgent problem in their neighbourhood. On a five-point scale, we asked them to indicate how prevalent the problem was. In both segregated areas, the most pressing issue is being littered, followed by the presence of drug users and dealers, particularly prominent in Tetemvár. The high proportion of troublemakers was ranked third, and the noise made by children and their truancy were likewise noted as problems in both settlements. In Bábonyibérc, the rate of those engaged in illicit trade and extortion is extremely high, while in Tetemvár, litter, alcohol consumption and drug use were particularly problematic.

The respondents were also asked about how much the residents helped each other. One in two people claimed that everyone mostly looked after themselves. At the same time, one in two thought that people in the neighbourhood helped each other in general and in case of trouble as well. In this regard, the rate of cohesion is slightly higher in Bábonyibérc.

Resources
(financial, material, psychological, social, as well as existing competencies of the population)

Let us first look at the material resources and the lack thereof.

The research intended to find out to what extent families were in debt, and if so, from whom, for what purpose, and what type of loan they had taken out.

	Total	Tetemvár	Bábonyibérc
Yes	25,7	18,5	31,9
No	74,3	81,5	68,1
Total	100,0	100,0	100,0

Table 2: Do you have a loan?
Source: own research

In Bábonyibérc, one in three families got a loan, either from others or from the bank, predominantly for purchasing and renovating their dwelling place or for purchasing a car. The sad fact is that many borrow money from the bank or a private person to be able to buy food.

One indicator of financial resources is the equipment of households with various articles and tools. Almost all the families surveyed have electricity, a mobile phone, a stove, separate beds and a colour TV.

In total, 85.5% of the households in the two segregated areas have sewage disposal. Drinking water is available to 63% of the residents in Tetemvár and 80% of the inhabitants of Bábonyibérc, while piped gas is available to 82% in Tetemvár and 61% in Bábonyibérc.

Consequently, housing conditions are better in Tetemvár because there is a higher proportion of sewage disposal, piped water and gas in the households. On the other hand, there are proportionally more bicycles, cars and computers owned by the residents of

Bábonyibérc, which underlines the fact noted earlier: there are more young people living in these households.

The questionnaire sought to explore material resources and opportunities as well, based on the following five questions:

- Has it happened in the past year that you were unable to pay your bill/loan on time? (%) (question 50.)
- Can you afford a family holiday that you have to pay for? (%) (question 51.)
- Can you afford to eat meat every other day? (%) (question 52.)
- In the case of an unexpected household expense, can you pay for it with your own money? (%) (question 53.)
- Can you heat your property properly and keep it warm in the winter cold? (%) (question 54.)

Questions 50 and 54 had a different context in the summer when the survey was conducted, and the rapidly escalating utility costs and the concomitant problems were not yet palpable. As indicated by the graphs and responses below, the residents of Bábonyibérc have experienced more problems. One in three households has difficulties paying bills or loans, two in three cannot afford to go on a holiday that they have to pay for, and one in two cannot afford to pay for an unexpected expense with their own money.

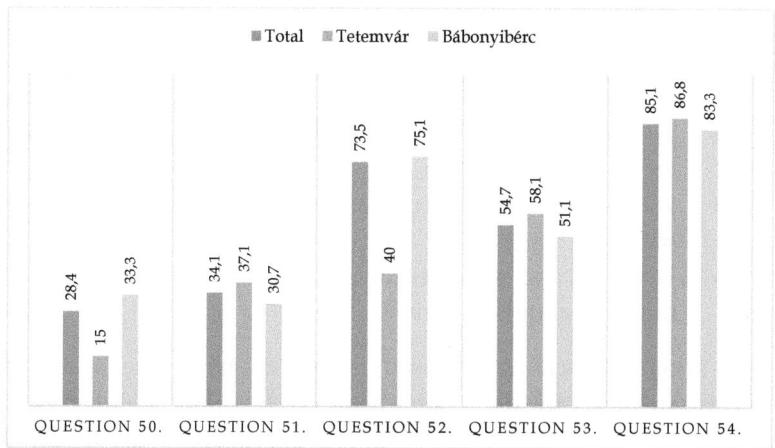

Figure 9: Answers to questions 50 to 54
Source: own research

The questionnaire also included the question "Have you ever worked abroad?" This query is highly important and is increasingly so in the present day, as a number of studies show that many of those living in rural and urban slums take the opportunity to work abroad temporarily in order to improve the financial situation of their family. Although COVID-19 greatly limited this opportunity as well, it is reemerging as the pandemic recedes. According to our survey, 13% of the inhabitants of Tetemvár and 10% of Bábonyibérc have experience in or are currently working abroad.

One important indicator of mental well-being is how satisfied individuals are with their lives and how happy they consider themselves. The respondents were asked to indicate their level of satisfaction and happiness on a scale of one to ten.

Overall, the people living in the two segregated areas could not be described as unhappy, as the average happiness level is 6.6. Contentment, which is a more long-term feeling and involves rational considerations, is 6.9. The responses also revealed that the residents of Tetemvár are happier and more content than those of the other segregated neighbourhood.

The questionnaire included questions to measure mental well-being with the help of the Beck Depression Inventory based on which the following correlations were found:

- The mental state of those in a relationship appears to be better.
- Women are more worried about their physical health than men.
- Divorced and widowed individuals are more likely to feel hopeless about the future.

Social interactions are based on trust in one another and such trust correlates with the mental health of a society, the degree of social integration, the quality of life and the sense of happiness and contentment of its citizens. Research in this area has consistently shown that the level of trust in Hungarian society is low and limited to a small circle (the immediate family and friends), and the level of trust in public institutions is not very high either.

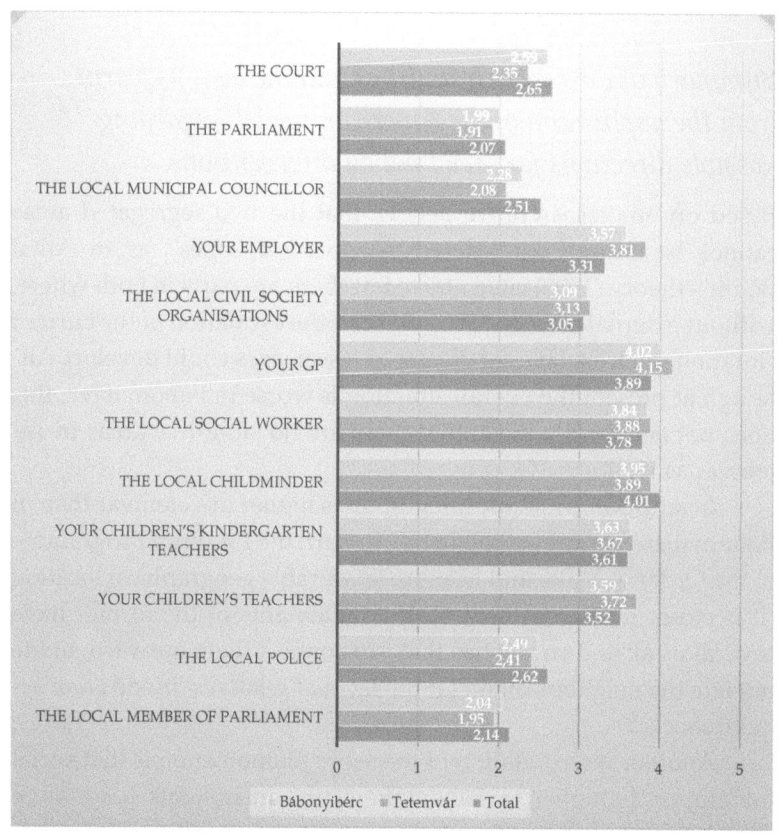

Figure 10: How much do you trust (on a scale of 1 to 5) the following?

Source: own research

Figure 10 shows that the inhabitants generally trust their local childminder, GP and social worker the most, while large-scale politics, the parliament and MPs are trusted the least. It appears that the people feel let down by big politics and can only trust the local people who provide various services.

The research also shows that 60% of people have a bank card and a personal email address, two-thirds can use a computer at a basic level and one-third have a driving licence.

Summary of the research findings and the lessons learnt from the application of the American model, regarding possible directions for social policy interventions

Based on our research, we believe that the two segregated areas cannot be entirely considered "depression zones" as in Antal Bőhm's theory (1992) cited above but there are parts in both where, without external intervention and with the escalation of the current situation, such enclaves of greater or lesser sizes could develop. Although at present the overall situation is worse in Bábonyibérc, this does not necessarily mean that there are no slum-like areas in Tetemvár as well.

In addition, systemic integration is higher in Tetemvár than in Bábonyibérc, meaning that due to, in part, the Presence Programme of the Order of Malta and its more favourable geographical location (it is closer to the city centre), the inhabitants of the former have several weak and strong ties that can connect them outward, to life outside the neighbourhood (at the level of relatives, friends and acquaintances).

Another interpretation of the same phenomenon is that social integration is higher in Bábonyibérc (the inhabitants have more friends in the neighbourhood, they attend community programmes more frequently, etc.) so they are less outwardly mobile. Connected to this, Bábonyibérc has a higher sense of public safety among its residents, while Tetemvár, being more permeable and less integrated, is perceived by its residents as more dangerous.

Both districts are characterised by a kind of present-oriented habitus (Stewart, 2001), also known in theoretical literature as a subculture of poverty. At the same time, this habitus is also a cognitive pattern and is associated with a lack of realistic plans for the future, a lack of clarity concerning and uncertainty about the concept of time, immediately using up all resources and, in general, a certain instant gratification.

At the same time, the inhabitants have a wide strategic repertoire of coping strategies for dealing with the precarity of their situation, including all four types described earlier (Lazarsfeld, 1929).

As mentioned above, one of the most widespread coping strategies of our time according to Piko (2002) is trying to overcome the stressful situation as rapidly as possible and with as little effort as possible, which, in several cases, can lead to the development of various addictions. This pattern can also be observed in the two segregated districts studied.

Based on the surveys, we registered 107 occupied properties in the area of Tetemvár delimited. We conclude that at present a maximum of 350 people may reside in the neighbourhood.

In the case of Bábonyibérc, 200 plots were found in the area delimited, 86 of which are occupied properties. Based on our estimations, the maximum number of residents is 300.

The two areas have broadly similar features in several aspects. For instance, two-thirds of the inhabitants moved to the district before 2000. They also show similarities in their ethnic composition, as one-fourth of the residents identify themselves as exclusively Roma (not Roma and Hungarian, nor exclusively Hungarian). In terms of age composition, the population is older in Tetemvár than in the other target area. The number of economically active residents is also higher in Tetemvár. In contrast, the Bábonyibérc community includes a larger young population and more families with several children.

In both segregated areas, nearly 80% of the residents live in their own real estate. In terms of infrastructure, Tetemvár is in a more favourable position and its inhabitants have fewer social problems in total than the residents of Bábonyibérc.

As asserted earlier, it is almost impossible to eliminate the phenomenon of urban slums from urban life. In the light of our research, we still firmly believe in this statement. Both our surveys and the relevant theoretical literature show that the most important reason for this is that the slum always has some socio-economic function for both its inhabitants and the environment (the local population and city leaders): adaptation and protection; integration (creating its own order and rules, spontaneous development regulated by the inhabitants), solidarity and capitalisation (the often illegally built public utilities are legalised over time).

It was also claimed that the inhabitants of urban slums do not form a homogeneous block but may differ in a wide range of social and individual characteristics, as illustrated by Seely's model from 1959 – this was likewise confirmed by our research.

Applying Seeley's model to our research, the residents of the two neighbourhoods may be classified as follows:

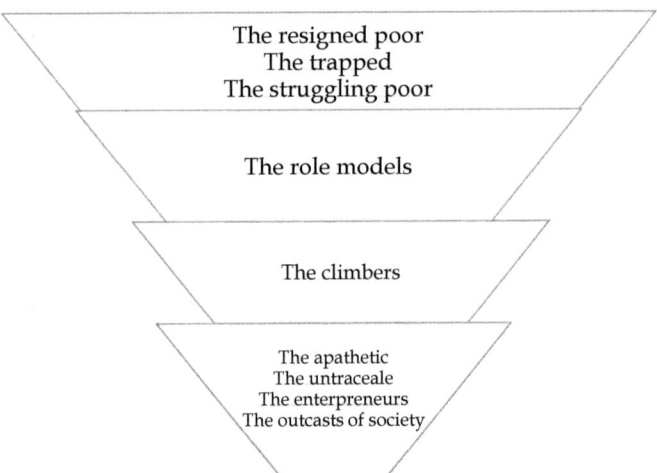

Figure 11: Classifying the population of the segregated areas based on the surveys

Source: own research

(Note: The typology was constructed by asking the interviewer after the questionnaire was taken to classify the family into the category considered most appropriate based on the twelve groups classified by Seeley. The figure shows each group of the classification according to the number of residents in the two settlements in decreasing order.)

Figure 11 shows that the so-called "resigned poor" form the largest block in the two segregated areas. They are the ones who consider their existence in the settlements as permanent and who live in constant destitution. They have almost come to terms with their situation. They generally conform to social norms and adapt to both the slum and the world outside simultaneously. They do not protest against their situation. They take care of their children and grandchildren. They may be starving by the end of the month, as they have scant resources for subsistence. They usually have some form of income. This group is hardly ever characterised by drinking or other deviances. The resigned poor enjoy their independence in this existence and are usually not willing to move elsewhere for the sake of a little comfort. Many of them are elderly or single mothers. They do not have the money, nor the motivation to leave the neighbourhood.

In their case, the role of social aid is to make life more comfortable in the slum by organising community activities and providing local social assistance.

The second largest group is "the trapped." These individuals predominantly moved here when the district was in a better state and are now incapable of moving away because their homes are worthless. They are the temporary residents of the settlement, which means that they would happily leave if they had the opportunity. They could be moved from the neighbourhood, possibly by providing them with good quality rental housing or cheaper properties outside the slum. Their lives, too, could be made more comfortable with the services described above.

The third most populous group is that of "the struggling poor." It is likely that at certain points in their lives, they lived outside the neighbourhood. Now they mainly live here. They are similar to the resigned poor but for their identification and most of their relationships outside the district, meaning that they have strong and weak ties outside the world of the slum. They pay their bills and try to obey the majority rules. As for their social and systemic integration, they also tend to gravitate towards life outside the slum. They can and are highly motivated to break with the help of social housing or other cheap housing elsewhere.

The next group consists of "the role models." They are like gurus, great old ones, wise men who know the drill and tell others how things are. They know the rules and thus play the role of informal leaders. The members of this group have no motivation to leave the slum and live there quite well, usually have income and are not in need. They view their life in the slum as an opportunity that also gives them prestige by integrating them into the local community. Therefore, their social integration is high, and their systemic integration is lower. Social programmes must take these role models into account. They need to be found and addressed, because having them on our side can ensure successful operation in the neighbourhood, as opposed to them acting as the 'gatekeepers' and hindering the success of intervention programmes.

"The climbers" are the fifth largest group, who see life in the slum as temporary and leave as soon as they can. They have savings, are hard-working and can think in the long term. They are often homeowners and diligent savers. Social programmes can help their outward aspirations by providing rental housing, buying their homes or showing them other housing alternatives outside the neighbourhood.

Finally, there are a larger number of "apathetic" inhabitants in the two segregated areas, who also need to be taken into account when organising social programmes. They resigned themselves to living in the slum permanently and are depressed or prone to depression. In terms of motivation and potential, this group is the most immobile one, its members are often apathetic alcoholics or addicts. They have been out of work for years and, in many cases, they neglect their children and homes. They may be in state care and on the edge of existence. From the aspect of social programmes, it is important for them to make their current situation more comfortable, as much as possible. For their children, family care and follow-up on the family is highly important.

References

Beck, U. (2003): *A kockázat-társadalom – Út egy másik modernitásba*. [Risk Society. Towards a New Modernity.] Budapest: Századvég Alapítvány.

Bőhm A. (1992): Depressziós zónák helyi társadalmai. [Local Societies of Depression Zones.] *Esély*, 2.

Castell, R. (2000): The Roads to Disaffiliation: Insecure Work and Vulnerable Relationships. *International Journal of Urban and Regional Research*. 24(3)

Havasi V. (2018): Még mindig szilánkos. Miskolc és a cigányság lakhatási ügyei az elmúlt harminc évben. [Still Fragmented: Miskolc and Housing for the Roma in the Past Thirty Years]. *Romológia*. 16 (1)

Helyi esélyegyenlőségi program. [Local Equal Opportunities Programme], 2021-2026. Miskolc Megyei Jogú Város Önkormányzata

Jahoda, M — Lazarsfeld, P. F. — Zeisel, H. (1999): *Marienthal — Szociográfiai kísérlet a tartós munkanélküliség hatásáról*. [Marienthal. The Sociography of an Unemployed Community.] Budapest: Új Mandátum Könyvkiadó.

Ladányi J. — Szelényi I. (2004): *A kirekesztettség változó formái*. [Changing forms of Exclusion]. Budapest: Napvilág Kiadó.

Lengyel G. (2009): Szilánkos mennyország — Szegénytelepek, cigánytelepek Miskolcon. [Fragmented Heaven: Poor neighbourhoods and Roma Slums in Miskolc]. *Beszélő*, 7-8.

Miskolc Megyei Jogú Város Önkormányzatának kezdeményezése: Munkacsoport a leszakadó városrészek integrációjának elősegítésére 2020-2021. Összefoglaló a munkacsoport munkájáról. [Initiative of the Municipality of Miskolc: Working Group for the Integration of Deprived Districts 2020-2021. Summary of the work of the working group]. Manuscript, 2021.

Miskolc Megyei Jogú Város településfejlesztési koncepciója (2014-2030). [Urban Development Concept of the Municipality of Miskolc, MMJV 2014. Manuscript.

Miskolc Megyei Jogú Város Integrált Településfejlesztési Stratégiája [Integrated Urban Development Strategy of the Municipality of Miskolc], 2014, 2018. Manuscript.

Márczis M. — Scharle Á. — Török Zs. (2024): 4IM Városi kezdeményezés az innovatív és integrált szociális szolgáltatásokért, foglalkoztatásfejlesztésért Miskolcon. Zárótanulmány. [Municipal Initiative for Innovative Integrated Interventions in Miskolc. Final Study] https://www.miskolc.hu/sites/default/files/egyszeru_oldal/beagyazhato_csatolmanyok/2024-07-03/82689/4im_e-konyv.pdf

Pikó B. (2002): *Egészségszociológia*. [Sociology of Health]. Budapest: Új Mandátum Kiadó.

Seeley, J. R. (1959): The Slum: Its Nature, Use, and Users. *Journal of the American Institute of Planners*, 25:1.

Stewart, M. (2001): "Depriváció, romák és "underclass" [Deprivation, the Roma, and the „Underclass"]. *Beszélő*, 7-8.

Szabó-Tóth K. (2005): Comparative study on the identity types of 'successful' Gypsies/Travellers in Hungary and in England. *European Integration Studies*, 4.

Szabó-Tóth K. (2004): Kiemelkedett cigányok (Gypsy/Travellers) etnikai identitásának jellegzetességei Angliában. [Characteristics of the Ethnic Identity of Gypsy/Travellers in England]. *Szociológiai Szemle*, 14.

Teller N. (2011): Adaptációs csapdák. Hipotézisek a romák lakásmobilitásáról, a 2010-es roma adatfelvétel lakásváltoztatási kérdéseire adott válaszok és a korábbi cigányfelvételek lakásmobilitási adatai alapján. [The Traps of Adaptation: Hypotheses on Roma Housing Mobility, Based on Responses to Issues of Moving Houses in the 2010 Roma Survey and Housing Mobility Data from Previous Roma Surveys. In Kurucz E. (szerk.): *Roma kutatások 2010. Élethelyzetek a társadalom peremén*. [Roma Studies 2010. Living on the Margins of Society]. Budapest: Nemzeti Család- és Szociálpolitikai Intézet.